Amira Badawey was born in Charlotte, N.C. At the age of seven she moved with her family to Cairo, Egypt. Amira always had a passion for reading and storytelling; she dreamt one day to write her own stories. After attending a writing class in NYU in 2013, Amira embarked on her own writing journey, based on capturing nuances from her surrounding environment. Drawn to stream of consciousness writing, Amira enjoys examining inner reflections of characters and their struggles with acceptance, belonging, and grief.

To Ahmed, Youseef and Zeina Moatz, may you always find the courage to be yourselves.

Amira S. Badawey

# NEVER BEEN

AUSTIN MACAULEY PUBLISHERS™
LONDON · CAMBRIDGE · NEW YORK · SHARJAH

**Copyright © Amira S. Badawey 2022**

The right of Amira S. Badawey to be identified as author of this work has been asserted by the author in accordance with Federal Law No. (7) of UAE, Year 2002, Concerning Copyrights and Neighboring Rights.

All rights reserved. No part of this publication may be reproduced, stored in a retrieval system, or transmitted in any form or by any means, electronic, mechanical, photocopying, recording, or otherwise, without the prior permission of the publishers.

Any person who commits any unauthorized act in relation to this publication may be liable to legal prosecution and civil claims for damages.

This is a work of fiction. Names, characters, businesses, places, events, locales, and incidents are either the products of the author's imagination or used in a fictitious manner. Any resemblance to actual persons, living or dead, or actual events is purely coincidental.

The age group that matches the content of the books has been classified according to the age classification system issued by the National Media Council.

ISBN – 9789948041344 – (Paperback)
ISBN – 9789948041351 – (E-Book)

Application Number: MC-10-01-9742468
Age Classification: 17+

Printer Name: iPrint Global Ltd
Printer Address: Witchford, England

First Published 2022
AUSTIN MACAULEY PUBLISHERS FZE
Sharjah Publishing City
P.O Box [519201]
Sharjah, UAE
www.austinmacauley.ae
+971 655 95 202

"Hello. Is this Mrs. Baldwin?"

"Yes."

"This is Jose. I'm the super from your daughter's building. We were cleaning out her apartment and found some of her stuff. We're supposed to throw out anything people forget, but I thought Zoe would like to have them. I tried to call her but she's not answering."

"I'm sorry, are you saying that Zoe has moved out of the building?"

"Yes ma'am. She moved out last month and left a box of stuff and some books. Do you want us to throw them out? That's what we are supposed to do anyway."

"No, please don't do that. I'll come and take a look. Can you just give me a few days?"

"Well, I don't know. We're supposed to start working on the apartment this week. The building manager isn't gonna like it if we delay."

"Jose, please. I'll be on the first flight to New York. Just a day or two. That's all I'm asking."

"I'll see what I can do. But I can't promise anything. If the boss comes over and sees them, we're gonna have to throw them out."

"I understand. Thank you for calling."

"No problem."

Patricia placed the phone back in its cradle on the kitchen wall. She was dazed from her conversation with Jose. She walked into the living room. Her husband, Kenneth, sitting in a beige recliner with their two chihuahuas, Samson and Delilah, was watching American Pickers on the History Channel. It took him a few minutes to notice Pat standing in the door way, gazing at the floor.

"What's the matter? Who was on the phone?" He asked.

"The superintendent from Zoe's building. He said she moved out a month ago and left some things behind."

"You didn't tell me she was moving. Did she get that apartment in Brooklyn?"

"I don't know. She didn't mention anything. I'm going to call her."

She reached for her cell phone and dialed her daughter's number. There was no answer. She logged onto her computer and tried Skype. Patricia and Zoe Skyped every day. She liked seeing Zoe's face while they talked. Zoe was offline. Patricia left her a message.

"Isn't she in Europe?" asked Ken.

"Yes. She'll be gone for a month. She said that she'll be off the grid."

Ken frowned inquisitively.

"No electronic devices, but she always checks her messages. Always. Why would she move out of her apartment? I don't like this."

"I'm sure it's nothing."

"I have to find a flight to New York."

"Well, now, wait a minute. Why are you going to New York?"

"To get her stuff."

"Pat, if she wanted those things, she would've taken them."

"The super said she left books. When have you ever known Zoe to throw away a book, nevertheless books? I'll sort through the items. If I find something I know she'd want, I'll ship them back here."

"Why didn't you ask the super to ship the books, instead of you going all the way to New York."

"I'm curious. I want to see her apartment."

"Fine. God knows you've already decided to go, regardless of my opinion. Do you want me to come along?"

"No."

Patricia took a JetBlue flight the following morning. She arrived at 12:30 noon and took a cab to Rockville Center on

Long Island. She checked in at the Hampton Suites and called Jose. They agreed to meet at three o'clock. With a few hours to spare, Patricia decided to explore the vicinity.

The hotel was situated on an inclination along Merrick Road, off Sunrise highway. Patricia put on her winter coat and headed outside. She walked the five blocks to the city center. It was early February. New York's cold wind seeped into her bones despite layers of clothes. She further insulated herself with gloves, a purple cashmere scarf Zoe gave her for Christmas, and wool stockings. The harsh weather hurt her arthritic joints. She blew into her cupped hands as she walked east on Sunrise. She turned right on Park Avenue. There was an assortment of bars and restaurants, a beaten-up AMC movie theater, ice-creme parlors, and a Starbucks. She crossed the street to indulge in a cup of coffee.

A year before, Patricia received a call from Zoe informing her that she was moving to New York. Zoe had been with her Chicago firm for twelve years, when she resigned. They had promoted her to Director of IT Projects. Patricia couldn't understand why her daughter would abruptly leave her job, sell her condo, and move to New York.

"I need a break. I can't do this anymore. I want to focus on other things besides work." Zoe told her mother.

This was all a surprise to Patricia. Zoe never had other interests beyond her career. Patricia often warned Zoe that she was forfeiting her personal life in sacrifice for her job. Zoe was a private person and Patricia didn't want to pry, she never asked Zoe about her romantic relationships.

Zoe had always been a bit of a tomboy. She inherited Patricia's amber curly hair. She kept it firmly pulled back in a tight braid, high on the crown of her head. She rarely wore makeup. "It feels like my face can't breathe," she told her mother. Her uniform throughout school and college was jeans, converse snickers, and dark cardigans with plaid shirts. On her sixteenth birthday, Patricia took Zoe to the gynecologist for birth control. As they left the doctor's office, Zoe murmured, "Don't worry mom, I won't have sex while in high school. My job is to study and get good grades." Zoe was focused on her education. She was an honor student and planned to study Computer Science. She did additional course work and extra curricula activities to leverage her application to the top programs in the country. She rewrote and edited her admittance essay repetitively, until she was happy with the draft. She practiced her responses to interview questions and carefully choose an appropriate outfit, a navy-blue pants suit with a crisp white oxford shirt and black Mary Jane's. She enrolled in the University of Illinois at Urbana-Champaign.

Zoe was a loner. She had one best friend, Alison. They met on the first day of preschool and remained close until the ninth grade when Alison's family moved to Portland. At first, they exchanged letters regularly and visited over summer breaks. Yet, they grew apart as they transitioned into adulthood. Their correspondence reduced to birthday cards and occasional phone calls. They last saw each other at Alison's wedding.

"I felt like a stranger, sitting there with her friends. They all know each other. I was the only outsider," Zoe commented.

Zoe hadn't spoken to Alison in seven years. At college, Zoe was friendly with everyone, but friends with no one. Classmates joined her study groups for her thorough notes and concise summaries but they didn't invite her to their parties. Patricia anxiously waited for Zoe to bring home a boy, or girl, to meet her and Ken. But that never happened. Patricia was happy when her daughter got a job offer while in graduate school. Although it kept her in Illinois, Patricia had hoped that Zoe would start living.

Zoe bought a condo two years after moving to Chicago. Her job required frequent traveling to Europe and Asia. Zoe dreaded those business trips. Flying was inconvenient because Zoe suffered from debilitating motion-sickness. She refused to take medication. "It makes me loopy," she told her mother. To compensate the burden of flying, Zoe appended vacation days to her trips. She explored new cities, visited museums, and experienced local cuisines.

Over the years, Patricia and Zoe maintained daily calls. It was an opportunity for Patricia to offload the burden of her day. Patricia continued to work at the age of sixty-nine. She taught fifth grade math. During their calls, Patricia complained about students' attitudes and dogmatic school administrations. She also updated Zoe on Ken's health.

"He's doing so much better, eating less sodium, and more fish. He likes Mahi, of all things. He has to go for three walks a day, now that we have the babies. We went to the mall yesterday for new pants. His old ones are too loose around the waist."

"That's nice," replied Zoe.

"How are things with you?"

"Fine. Everything's fine."

"Work's okay?"

"Yes. Busy, busy, busy."

"Are you traveling soon?"

"No."

As she stared out of the sunlit window at Starbucks and sipped a cappuccino, Patricia realized that Zoe never really shared much. Patricia did most of the talking while Zoe simply listened to her mother's grievances and answered her questions.

Patricia arrived at Zoe's apartment building. Jose was waiting for her in the lobby. He was short and bold. He spoke with a slight Columbian accent.

"Hi. Nice to meet you. Thank you for coming so soon. We really have to clear the apartment. Your daughter was very nice and kind. Always saying good morning and hello. She always offered me coffee, when I went to fix something. Too bad she had to move."

He chatted as they waited for the elevator. Zoe's apartment was on the third floor. Patricia preferred to take the stairs. Nevertheless, she patiently waited next to Jose while the elevator descended. She observed the building's details. It was a simple structure, with nondescript features and clean straight lines. The exterior landscape, although dilapidated by recent snow, was well maintained. The entry way was a standard off-white affair, with a neutral brown tiled floor. A generic round wooden table and vase stood in the middle. The predominate scent was laundry mingling with the smell of cooking emanating from various kitchens.

Jose held the elevator door open for Patricia. "Zoe never took the elevator, always the stairs. Even when she do laundry, always the stairs. She'd say, 'This is the only exercise I get'. Please tell her I say hello."

"I will," replied Patricia.

"Ah, here we are."

They walked out of the elevator and down a hallway to unit 3S. Jose unlocked the avocado green door. The apartment smelled of bleach and lemon Pledge.

"Zoe clean everything before she leave. Bathroom is scrubbed cleaner then when she moved in. She even cleaned the refrigerator and stove. Everything so clean," he said.

A short entryway led to an open living space. To the right was a large room, twelve by thirty feet. Two windows overlooked South Park Avenue. The blinds were pulled up. Sunlight shone onto the polished hardwood floor. Across the entryway was a galley kitchen with French doors. Zoe left oil wick air freshener plugged into power outlets throughout the space. A strong hint of vanilla mixed with stale bleach suffocated Patricia. She opened a window and inhaled the fresh crisp winter air. She turned to address Jose.

"Thank you for letting me in. I will sort through the items. If I find anything important, I'll take it with me. Feel free to discard the rest."

Jose left her with instructions to lock the door when she was done, and to place the key in the mail box next to his office downstairs in the basement.

In the center of the living room, Patricia surveyed seventy-two books, three journals, and a MacBook Air. A shopping trolley stood next to the kitchen door. Patricia walked around, opening closets and browsing for other items Zoe might have forgotten. She checked kitchen cabinets and drawers. She looked inside the oven and freezer. Everything was vacant. The outside of the cabinets, the backsplash and counter tops, all reeked with bleach. The bedroom and bathroom were no different. Every corner, every shelf and every door were void of evidence that Zoe inhibited the apartment for a year. Nothing was left behind, not even dust bunnies.

Patricia went back to the living room. She stared at the neat pile of discarded items. It was obvious that Zoe didn't forget them by mistake. Patricia picked up one of the books. It was *Actors Anonymous* by James Franco. It was a signed copy. Patricia recalled Zoe telling her that she waited in the rain for two hours simply to realize later that the event was standing room only. Franco arrived late and stayed for twenty minutes to read a couple of paragraphs. *Why would Zoe leave her signed copy behind?*, Patricia wondered. She opened the book. It contained a written note in Zoe's hand.

*To whoever finds this book,*

*I hope you enjoy reading it as much I did. When you're done, leave it on a park bench so that other people can have the opportunity to enjoy it as well.*

*Sincerely,*
*Zoe Baldwin*

Patricia picked up another volume. It, too, had the same message. They all did. *Maybe a friend was supposed to collect the books and give them away*, Patricia thought. It didn't seem possible, given that Zoe had handed in her keys when she canceled her lease. Patricia gathered the journals and laptop. She returned to the hotel.

Back at her room in The Hampton Suites, Patricia left the journals on the console next to the flat screen TV. She avoided them for the rest of the evening. She busied herself with a shower and dinner. She microwaved a Stouffer's Mac and Cheese. It was Zoe's favorite. She later called Ken.

"I'm sure Zoe has a good reason for leaving those things in the apartment. Wait until she's back and she'll explain everything," he told Patricia.

"Something's not right, Kenneth. Why would she leave her laptop? She loved that thing. She treated it like a pet, even called it Arnold."

"Pat, she's a grown woman. Stop worrying."

Unable to resist temptation much longer, Patricia decided to read Zoe's diaries. She felt guilty for infringing on her daughter's privacy, yet she couldn't rid herself of an ominous notion that the journals contained an explanation to Zoe's odd behavior over the previous year. She settled under the duvet with the three beautifully bound books, one in tiffany blue, another with metallic butterflies and the last was tomato red. She removed the elastic band and commenced reading her daughter's inner most thoughts. She was thankful for Zoe's precise penmanship and organized composition. She started with the first entry, dating back to January 2012.

# January

I went straight to a Hudson bookstore upon arriving at JFK, and bought this dairy. It makes sense to start my journal now, on the twenty-ninth of January. It's a new beginning that warrants its own journal. I'm so tired, not sure why. I'll take a nap when I get to the hotel.

I checked in at The Hampton Inn and Suites. It was either here, the Best Western down the street, or Holiday Inn further west. The corridors at the Best Western are opened to the street. I wouldn't have been safe staying there. The Holiday Inn is too far away from the train station. So, Hampton Inns and Suites it is. I opened the closet door. It's a sliding mirror panel. I keep it open without eating away from the crapped space of my hotel room. I checked under the beds. I took a warm shower and left the bathroom door open. I don't like closed doors and concealed spaces. They make me anxious. You never know what's lurking in the darkness. I turned on all the lights and slept for five and half hours.

It's already dark outside. I'm hungry. The hotel doesn't serve food. Nearby restaurants are closed. It is eleven o'clock at night. I'll go to the King Kullen next door and pick up some snacks.

\*\*\*

I woke up at nine this morning. It's still early in the day, but it's a late start. Why am I jet lagged? There's only a two hour difference between Chicago and the east coast. Or is it three? I can't think. I should know this. I must get out of bed. There is so much to do.

I was fortunate to find an apartment in Rockville Center. Last November, when I came over to interview for the position, they recommended the Hampton Inn as a nearby hotel because I didn't want to drive. I can't drive anymore. My mind won't stay still. It wanders off. People say that driving becomes second nature. It's true. I don't need to think about driving, while I'm driving. Yet, I still need to focus and it's difficult to focus with a mind that rapidly bounces from one thought to the next. My mind focuses on anything rather than the surrounding cars. At a traffic light once, it flew away with a red winged blackbird, wondering where its nest was, whether it flew in a flock or alone. I peered over the steering wheel to get a better view and lifted my foot off the brakes. The car rolled into intersecting traffic. The horns of passing cars brought me back to reality. I safely stopped the car before it collided with another. One morning, I was late for work because my mind followed a little girl in an orange rain coat to school. It couldn't decide if she was in elementary or middle stage. No, I can't drive a strange car in a strange city. At least in Chicago, the car knew its way. It got me to where I needed to be. But not in New York. So, I stayed in the Hampton Inn, in Rockville Center. It was a few blocks away from the train station along the Babylon Line. From there I took the Long Island Rail Road to Freeport, and a five-dollar cab to the office. When they offered me the job, I knew right away that I wanted to live in Rockville Center. I told my realtor to find me a one-bedroom unit on the last floor of an apartment building. She tried to convince me to look outside Rockville Center. She offered apartments in Westbury. They were new constructions with stainless steel appliances. "It only takes twenty-five minutes to get to Freeport. Just drive south on the Meadowbrook Parkway," she said. But I knew I couldn't drive, at least not now. So, I insisted on Rockville Center. I saw a couple of studio apartments. They were sad to look at, with yellowing walls and green carpeting. The kitchenettes were an afterthought, tagged on in haste. They reminded me of the play sets we had in preschool. The closet and micro-bathroom stood side-by-side, right there in the open space. No hallway. No privacy. Both units were on the ground floor, at street level, with cars and pedestrians zooming by. No, I couldn't stay in a studio. The realtor showed me another apartment on North Forrest Avenue. It was the last unit in a two-story building. It had an eat in kitchen. I immediately saw myself sitting at a round table next to the long rectangular window, drinking coffee in my PJs and slippers. The living room over looked a court yard. A large Pine Oak stood outside its window. The bedroom was quaint and quiet. Yet, the apartment was seven blocks from the train station and a mile away from the nearest supermarket. "You can have groceries delivered," said the realtor. "You can park your car in the lot across Sunrise. It only costs two hundred dollar a year." But I don't drive and I am living on Long Island. Can I say 'living,' when I've only been here for less than twenty-four hours. I suppose the proper term is 'moved to Long Island.' Yes, I have moved to Long Island and I can't survive here without driving. At the end, I decided on a one-bedroom apartment on South Park Avenue. It's a ten-minute walk to the train station. There's a laundry room in the basement, a Starbucks and movie theater down the street. It is a perfect fit.

My new job starts on the fifth of February. I only have seven days to get settled in.

I'm going to Ikea today. I've never been to Ikea before. Is that ironic or just sad? I'm going to the store in Hicksville. It'll take me two buses to get there. Maybe I should rent a car. I should try to drive. According to Google maps, it's eighteen miles away. I could go to the one in Brooklyn, but they don't deliver to Rockville Center. Maybe I should just purchase the furniture online. No. No. I need to see the pieces for myself. Touch them, to see if they are sturdy. Sit in them, to see if they are comfortable. I must go.

\*\*\*

I hate Ikea. I shall have traumatizing dreams about Ikea. I don't mind the nightmares, for Ikea is my living hell. I got lost in Ikea. I had a panic attack in Ikea, having failed to find my way out of the labyrinth of beds, couches, chairs, tables, endless arrays of cushions, linen, and towels. I never want to walk into another Ikea for as long as I live. I never want to traverse the concrete floors of their warehouse or navigate a flatbed full of boxes.

Despite the dismaying experience, I succeeded in buying a full-size bed, mattress, and dresser. The dresser weighed ninety pounds and was packed into a single box. I couldn't lift it on my own. I left my flatbed in the middle of the warehouse and searched from someone to help me. After fifteen minutes, I finally located a shop assistant. Yet, someone pouched the flatbed. I had to walk to the front of the warehouse for a new one. I demanded that the assistant, Chad, accompany me to the designated racks and help me with the boxes. He acquiesced, for he saw the tears of despair teetering on my eyelids. I thanked him with a big hug. I arranged for the boxes to be delivered today.

The realtor met me this morning at eight. She let me into the lobby and gave me a quick walkthrough, exhibiting which key opens which door. The small chrome one is for the front lobby door. The large brass key is for the back entrance leading to the parking lot. The silver key unlocks the apartment door. I'm sitting on the kitchen floor, with my back resting against the sink cabinet, waiting for the furniture and cable company. It's only 8:40. It's going to be a long day of idle nothingness. I should find a book store.

The cable guys were the first to arrive. There was two of them. I offered them bottled water but they declined. They went about, drilling and installing fiberoptic cables. They were very efficient. It only took them forty-five minutes to setup a router and two TV receivers, one in the living room and another in the bedroom. The furniture arrived while they were still here. A dolly rolled four medium boxes into the bedroom. I purchased the tools required to assemble the furniture yesterday from Ikea. I got a hammer, pliers, and a pink electric screw driver with interchangeable bits. It appealed to my feminine side, for I am an independent strong woman who will assemble her own furniture. Ikea placed these items conveniently next to the cash register, a reminder that the torture continues. I asked the delivery guy to rest the mattress against the wall in the hallway outside the bedroom door. I tipped him and he left.

***

I hate Ikea.

I'm back at the hotel. It has been a very long day. After the cable guys left, I set about to put together my new bed. The first page of the instruction manual was an omen of things to come. A rudimentary cartoon informed me that I'll need a buddy to help piece the puzzle together. I chose to ignore this warning, convinced that my intellect will find a workaround to my buddy-less state. I took out the various parts and laid them on the floor, mirroring their alignment in the manual. I had panicked and selected a unit with extra storage, a platform bed with four embedded drawers. I am living in New York after all. One can never have too much storage in New York. There were forty-six pieces, thirty-eight bits, thirty washers, and a hundred-and-sixty-eight screws.

I picked up the long rectangular side board and balanced it between my legs to keep it up right. I wedged a narrow footboard into the allotted section. In my own hellish version of twister, I successfully contoured my body and reached for the pink screw driver, without releasing the interlocked panels. My lips curved in a smug smile. I told myself, "I can do this." I secured the correct screws in place. Leaning over the pseudo structure, sweat pooled onto the lens of my eyeglasses. I blinked to clear my vision. My back cramped. Yet, I was adamant. I took a deep breath to regain my composure. And I huffed and I puffed, and the whole thing came tumbling down. The structure fell apart with a loud thud. Screws ricocheted off the floor. I tried and failed twice before giving up entirely. I called an assembly company. They gave me an appointment in two days.

I walked back to the hotel, with nothing to show for this long tiring day. I took a hot shower to calm my strained muscles. I put on my purple bathrobe, with embroidered butterflies. I was too tired to get dressed. I'm comatized in bed and can barely move. My new orthopedic mattress is propped up against a wall, warping. I should have laid it on the floor and slept on it. But I don't have any pillows, sheets, or covers. I must go shopping tomorrow. But now, I will sleep.

***

# February

OMG. I hate that expression, as much as I hate the word Meta, but I'm too tired to write full phrases. So, OMG. The last few days were an endless collage of shopping trips, cleaning, and unpacking. I have finally moved in the apartment on Park Avenue. The majority of it stands bare, yet my new bed and dresser grace the bedroom. My mattress lays atop the platform bed, snugly covered in new sheets. I'm laying atop the mattress, pajama clad, and tucked underneath the covers. My body's still cool from the shower. My hair is dripping shampoo infused droplets down my back. I can feel every muscle in my body. They ache. I have basted myself with Bengay to accelerate the effect of the warm message of the shower head. I smell of eucalyptus. I am too tired to care that the smell will infuse my new mattress cover and duvet.

The assembly company sent a team of five. They came by yesterday to put the furniture together. It took them twenty minutes to build the dresser and bed. They worked in tandem, without referring to the instruction manual. Like street performers, they worked in silence, each doing his part and trusting his team members to do theirs. I felt very inadequate, given that I fumbled for over ninety minutes and was unsuccessful in attaching two wooden boards together. Apparently, I had placed the side board upside down. That's why the screws wouldn't fasten securely.

I went to Radio Shack on Thursday to buy a small 32-inch TV set for the bedroom. I carried it to the apartment. It wasn't heavy. My arms ached from extending them the width of the box while carrying it for four blocks. I was thankful for the elevator because I didn't have to carry it up three flights of stairs. I gently placed it on the floor in the living room and went to the bathroom to wash my face. I realized that I didn't have any soap or towels. I turned the faucet clockwise and let the water run through my fingers. I cupped my hands and splashed my face with cold water. It dripped off my chin as I looked at my reflection in the mirror. *Of course, I don't have any plates, pots, pans. I don't have a vacuum, mop, cleaning supplies*, I reminded myself. I packed only one suitcase of clothes when I left Chicago. Everything else was either sold or given away. I even abandoned my books. I made a rash decision in a moment of emotional weakness, and now I am baring the consequences of my stupid choices. I stared into my void eyes. "Get your shit together," I shouted at the reflection.

When I got back to the hotel, I called Enterprise and rented a midsize sedan. They delivered it within forty minutes. I made a shopping list of items and googled nearby stores. There was a shopping center in Oceanside, three miles south of Rockville Center. It had a Marshall's, Kohl's, Bed Bath and Beyond, and Staples. It took multiple trips to purchase all the times on the list. I couldn't fit everything in the car all at once.

I checked out of the hotel this morning. I arrived at the apartment at nine o'clock. I scrubbed every inch in the kitchen and bathroom. I swept the floors and polished them before placing area rugs in the empty space, complying with the building's rule of covering eighty percent of the hard wood. I setup a coffee machine and small toaster oven in the kitchen. I made one final trip before leaving the car in the hotel's parking lot. I shopped for groceries at King Kullen. I stocked up on laundry detergent, hand soap, tooth paste, toilet paper, and microwavable dinners.

What am I doing? Is this insane? How can I do this on my own? Moving is tiring, especially when there's no one to help. I've never done anything like this before, not alone. When I went off to college, my mother told me what and how to pack. My parents flew with me to Illinois. They drove me to campus and helped me settle in. They stayed for the weekend to make sure I had everything I needed. Before leaving, they took me out for pancakes and groceries. Aaron was there when I moved to Chicago. We shared an apartment. When he and Diane moved to Dallas, I drove them to the airport. I always had Sylvia. I should have let her help me. It would have been nice to have an extra pair of hands. But, no, I can't accept her help. This is something I have to do on my own. But it's hard. It's so hard. I'm tired of having to be strong all the time. What is the alternative? If I had a child, I couldn't afford the luxury of momentary weakness. I'd have to be strong for the both of us, always. I can't bring a child into this world, only to neglect her. What if I am not strong enough? Who'll take care of the child? And what if it returns? Maybe the unconditional love of a child will keep it at bay. The responsibility of another will keep me strong. I'll never know for sure. Should I chance it with a child involved? How nice it must feel to have the peace of mind that someone out there will take care of you. Yet, no one's here. It's only me. I'm all I have.

This year is going to cost me greatly. So, I've decided it'll be a year. My salary is comparable to the market's rate. Fifty-six thousand is a decent pay for a project coordinator, but it's barely enough to cover rent and utilities. I'll have to use my savings to pay for all other expenses.

\*\*\*

I survived the first week as a project coordinator. It is a mindless job. I collect daily status reports from project managers and aggregate the data into an overall update. I compile missing documentation and make sure that everything is filed properly. I have no external customers, no deliverable, no responsibilities, no worries. My mind is free to wander in every direction, unconstrained by work.

Everyone is very nice and pleasant. They introduced themselves but didn't linger to pry. I share a work space with Melanie. She's nice, if a bit chatty. She's young, early twenties. She provides an ongoing social media commentary of her day, "I'm going to get a cup of coffee." "My butt hurts from sitting down." "I'm so hungover." I acknowledge these posts with constipated smiles. I'd much rather shout, I DON'T GIVE A FUCK, but I don't. She doesn't direct her updates to me when I wear my head phones. So, I have taken to leaving them on all day, even when I'm not listening to anything. Under this guise, I eavesdrop on her conversations. Last Friday, she made plans with her boyfriend. They were meeting after work. She'd intended to spend the night at his place. I wonder if Mike is sleeping with Sara. Maybe they had been sleeping together all along. Stop it. I'm being unfair. Her revealing outfits are not an indication of promiscuity. Maybe he's back with his former girlfriend. He never spoke about her. I wonder what's she like. He didn't even mention her name. Maybe he didn't have a girlfriend. He probably paid for sex. Stop it. Stop it.

I'm still getting used to the change of pace. My current existence is more base than tempo. I work from eight to four, Monday through Friday. I don't stay after hours or work on weekends. I am not obligated to check e-mails when I'm not in the office. I have so much leisure to do with as I please. I'm not sure how to utilize these superfluous hours. I need to find a bookstore. That's the only downside to Rockville Center. There aren't any bookstores, neither big chains nor independent ones.

***

My body woke up this morning at 5:24 am. The same time I get up every day. My inner clock cannot distinguish between weekdays and weekends. When it's time to get up, it gets up. It's a sunny cold winter day. Heavy clouds scatter the skies. We're expecting a dusting of snow. I'm perfectly insulated in my boots and North Face coat. Moving around is a challenge, but stabilizing my stance without falling is good exercise for my core.

I passed by Starbucks on the way to the train station. I ordered my regular drink, tall Pike Place in a grande cup. The four-ounce difference is the perfect allowance of nonfat milk. It has become a daily ritual. Anne and Marie are the weekday

Baristas. John and Lilo work weekends. Ryan is always there in the evenings. I usually sit next to the door where I get a clear view of the entire shop. I watch people stand in line, waiting to place their orders. I spy on their conversations and envy their laughter. My regular spot was occupied today, so I sat in another table. My back was to the crowd as I faced the large glass wall overlooking Park Avenue. Eight o'clock is early for a Saturday morning. There's sparse traffic, both cars and pedestrians. The city is still asleep. Across the street is Press 195. They serve panini sandwiches and craft beer. They have a live band every Thursday night. I should check it out one day. But they'll probably sit me at the bar. I look like a toddler, climbing up bar stools. Every date I went on, there weren't many, I'd stand at the bar waiting to be seated. My feet ached from the strain of seven-inch stilettos, but pain is invisible to others. The same is not true for the humiliation of getting on and off stupidly high bar stools.

\*\*\*

I'm in Heaven. I had a wonderful time yesterday. Long Island did get a dusting of snow. Walking back to the apartment was tricky. But New York City was beautiful, absolutely beautiful.

I took the LIRR to Penn station, then the N train from Herald square. I got off at Union square. It was 9:30. The sun peeked out from behind clouds. The park was packed with all sorts of families. Where Times Square is the intersection of humanity, stand there long enough and someone from every country in the world will pass by, yet Union Square is where families of every ethnicity congregate. I walked out of the subway station and selected a vacant bench under the shade of a tree. I closed my eyes and raise my face to salute the sun as it continued to ascend from the east. I felt the breeze of the wind. I felt the warm rays of the sun. I heard words spoken in every language known to man. I smiled and sat there for half an hour, observing and absorbing my surroundings. I crossed the street and entered Barnes and Noble.

Bookstores are my haven. I walk between the high bookshelves, browse volumes, and peek at the selection of other readers. I pick up random books, turn to a random page and read. If I'm captivated by the words, I buy the book. I don't find such pleasures with online purchases. I like holding the binds in my hand and flicking through the pages with my fingers, feeling them tickle the ridges of my prints. I like to inhale the aroma of paper and ink. I savor the convenience of reading a book on the toilet, in the subway, at the park, and on the train. I like licking my fingers to turn the page. I like earmarking my favorite passages and writing in the margins. Bumpy pages stained with tears, drips of coffee and food grease show that a book was loved and well used. They tell the story of the relationship between the book and the reader.

After I was done with Barnes and Noble, I walked south to The Strand. Their floor to ceiling shelves crammed with books exuded a sense of claustrophobia. Shop assistants were friendly and well informed, but tourists crowded the book lined corridors. I had to turn sideways to pass. I decided to return early morning next weekend and enjoy the space unadorned with people. I walked outside without purchasing any items and reviewed the elaborate window displays, the store's vintage red and white awning and the mobile carts of used books piled along the sidewalk of Twelfth street.

Still on my literary high, I walked further south towards Houston. The crowd morphed into Tall Young Hipsters. They talked loudly as they rushed to their destinations. Independent shops disappeared. Every commercially known brand cordoned Broadway. I threaded a zigzag path between the bunched-up shoppers traversing the sidewalk. Withdrawal symptoms manifested as the crowds grew denser. I turned left on Prince to escape. The pace subdued. Brunch commenced in an array of quaint bistros and cafes. People lounged on corner benches. Families and dog lovers occupied the scenery once again.

I came cross a few more independent books stores. Legacy shops like The Strand and Book Court are New York landmarks. Their lofty halls host eclectic events diverse with arts and literature. These establishments are littered with tourist garnering bragging rights. Younger generations of bookstores occupy smaller footprints and use the space more economically with clean minimalist designs. They keep the focus on the books. I browsed the offerings of two more stores, further augmenting my purchases with additional books, stationary, and periodicals. I continued east. At the corner of Mott Street I saw a huge glass window framed with pistachio colored wood. Pastel colored letter spelled 'Cupcakes'. I walked in. The shop was long and narrow. The display counters were on the left. Small round tables, large enough for two, stood to the right. I walked along the counter, surveying the goodies. First came the tarts and brownies, then cake slices and pudding cups, and finally individual cupcakes. I ordered a red velvet cupcake and Earl Grey tea. I sat at an empty table and devoured the food. The shop was a sanctuary from the outside world. No music played on the sound system. Everyone was hunched over their tables, engaged in hushed conversations. The tranquility was interrupted by the click clank of China and cutlery. An occasional ringtone chimed. But the atmosphere remained serene.

It was a beautiful day, and now I have my books.

\*\*\*

I didn't notice that it was Valentine's Day today. I had a busy day at work. We lost one of our servers. It took four hours to setup a new one. I had to restore documentation and project information to the new server from last week's backup. I updated the lagged data from reports locally stored on my machine. We had a meeting to recap the events of the day. We discussed lessons learnt and planned for preventative actions. I left the office at 7:30 PM. Charles, my boss, drove me to the train station. I waited on the platform because the ticket office closes at five. It was cold and dark. The platform was deserted with the exception of a young man with blond dreadlocks and an obese old woman. I pulled my cap as far down as possible to cover my ears. I scrunched up my shoulders to pack my scarf tighter around my neck. I blew into my gloved hands. I surrendered to the freezing wind and retired to the heated enclosure located mid-way down the platform. I pulled the heavy door open. A mixture of urine, alcohol, and putrefied air assaulted my sinuses. I took a step back and forcefully inhaled clean platform air before entering the space. Metal benches lined the walls of the long rectangular structure. Two doors stood at both ends. Glass windows extended above the benches, giving me a clear view of the tracks. The room was dimly lit with fluorescent lights. One of the lightbulbs flickered. I stood next to the door to make a quick exit once the stench got too intense to endure. I glanced at my watch every thirty seconds, willing the train to be on time. The PA system finally announced the arrival of the 8:05 westbound train to Penn station.

    I continued standing on the train. It's only a six-minute ride between Freeport and Rockville Center, not worth the hassle of selecting a free seat and sitting down. It started to drizzle as I walked south on Park Avenue. I pulled the hood of my coat over my head and bowed down to shield my glasses from the rain. I was preoccupied with work, pondering on additional contingencies, then reminding myself that I am not in charge. Resolving issues are no longer my responsibility. I execute the plans of others. Bars and restaurants were busier than usual. I lifted my head and looked up. A couple in front of me were huddled under an umbrella, holding hands, and leaning towards each other. I noticed another couple, hurrying into a restaurant. Across the street, a man standing next to a parked car held an umbrella up as he helped a woman out of the passenger's side. Still oblivious to the date, I assumed Tuesday was date night in Rockville Center. None of the establishments along Park Avenue displayed traditional red, pink, and heart decorations associated with Valentine's Day. They simply exhibited exceptionally high number of patrons, divided into amorous couples of two.

    I was propped up in bed, watching TV and eating dinner when my phone chimed. It was a text message. Unable to resist a beckoning phone, I instinctively reached for the device and pressed read. It was a message from my mother. Three words flashed on the screen, Happy Valentine's Day. This was my mother's reply to a text I sent her a week ago, informing her of my new mobile number. Typical Patricia. She won't call, if I don't call. She will, however, passive aggressively send texts, such as this one, to guilt me into calling her. I had no desire to talk to Patricia and hear her complain about work or Aunt Linda, to hear her criticize my move to New York, to hear her say that I'm wasting my life. I'm not ready for that. Not now. I checked my inbox to see if I had any messages from Mike. There were none. How can he text me when he doesn't have this number. Wasn't that the reason for a new phone, to avoid contact with Mike. I checked my personal e-mail. Nothing, just spam from eHarmony and Match.com reminding me that a special someone is out there waiting for me on their dating websites. I checked Facebook, hoping to find a long declaration of love, but Mike doesn't have a Facebook account. Why am I doing this? I knew there would be no messages from him on any medium, yet I continued to build up hope. I'm pursing false aspiration that Mike will come back to me, when he wasn't mine to begin with.

    I sense the darkness clouding my heart and mind. I don't want to feel like this any longer. I don't want to cry. I don't want to ache. I don't want to long for Mike. I try to push it away, but to no avail. I will never know how it feels to have someone be thankful for my every heartbeat. The thought of me will never bring genuine happiness to someone. No one will mourn my death. No one will ache with desire for me. I will never know the vanity of being loved.

    I must shun these thoughts. But the darkness festers on my pain and sorrow. It's growing inside me. I mustn't revert to that place. It took me seven years to climb out. I can't weather it again. I won't survive.

    I was neglected, rejected by the world. I had an emotional need to discharge my suffering. But, to whom? The fear of dying alone burdened my thoughts. My mother argued that I was focusing too much on my career at the expense of my personal life.

"Living is about finding the right balance," she'd say. "You have to want it as much as you want to succeed professionally."

I coveted it even more. I didn't know how to make it happen.

"Remember Ryan. He was a sweet boy. If you had simply agreed to go out on a date with him, you would have been happily married with two kids by now. He and his wife have bought a new house. She doesn't work. He pays for everything. Everything. That could have been you."

I talked to Sylvia. She iterated how lucky I was to do with my life as I pleased, making decisions without considering others, and not being bothered with a husband and children who demand my full attention. "You don't have to flee to the laundry room to enjoy a few minutes of peace and quiet. The grass is always greener. Take it from someone who's on the other side. Enjoy your freedom while you can," she said.

I had a good life. I knew that. I lived in an amazing city. I was paid handsomely to do a job for which I was passionate. I traveled and saw the world. I was thankful for the life I had, but I wanted something different. There was nothing I had that I wouldn't have given up for a family.

I was thirty when it first happened. I was numb, operating on autopilot, working, exercising, cooking, reading. But I wasn't invested in any of it. I couldn't sleep, no matter how hard I tried. I cultivated the habit of keeping the TV on at night during my first business trip. I couldn't fall asleep in a strange hotel room. I'd wake up in the middle of the night, startled at the unfamiliar surroundings. The ambient sounds of news channels were my lullaby. The habit carried over to my bedroom. Within eighteen months of that first trip, I had a twenty-one-inch flatscreen installed on the wall opposite my bed. But the muted tones of nightly news didn't put me to sleep anymore. Neither did infomercials, nor sitcom reruns. I'd lay in bed staring at the ceiling. I'd get up and clean, or work on reports. I kept a journal as an outlet for my emotional neediness. Recalling the day on paper bored my mind to a snooze. I enjoyed a few hours of sleep. Work didn't suffer from my lack of rest, but my body did. I was constantly tired. I had headaches and neck pains. That's when the darkness slowly crept in. My only solace was a hook in the middle of the ceiling in my bedroom. I'd close my eyes and see the image of my body swinging from a noose tied to the hook. I'd calm down and fall asleep.

\*\*\*

It's been a quiet day. Most days are quiet. I overheard Melanie give a detailed recollection of the Valentine's date she had with James, her boyfriend. I was in a bathroom stall, when she walked in with Liz. I tried to concentrate on my toilet duties and avoid listening to their conversation, but my bowels were shy with other people in hearing distance. I coughed to signal that someone else was in there and could hear their sexually explicit talk, but this didn't deter them. I exited the stall. They silently watched me wash my hands and walk out.

As I was collecting my things to leave for the day, Charles came by my desk.

"Zoe, a bunch of us are heading over to Kasey's for a drink. Why don't you come along?"

"Thank you, but I don't drink."

"Oh come on. It'll give you a chance to get to know everyone. Besides, you can have a soda or ginger ale or something."

"Again, thank you, but I'm sorry, I can't go."

"Suit yourself. Let me at least give you a lift. Kasey's just down the street from your apartment."

"That's very kind of you Charles, but I'm not going home." I lied.

What's the point of knowing them? People assume an inquisitive nature when they meet someone for the first time, especially in social settings. Having drinks is a euphemism to pry into my personal life. I'd have to entertain a game of twenty questions, "Where'd you live before moving to New York?"; "What did you do before joining the company?" "Has your family settled in nicely? Oh, no family, just you."

Why do I have to get to know them better? They are my colleagues. We tolerate each other between the hours of nine and five, and forget one another outside the office. The majority of the team have been with the company since the beginning. They have known each other for over ten years. I'd be like the awkward cousin, visiting from out of town. I suppose I am to blame for being awkward. "You are a party ghost. Your presence is felt although you remain invisible." Mike said to me the first time we went to a party together. It is true, I'm not the partying type. I loathe small talk. I think it is unnecessary and a complete waste of breath, meaningless jibber jabber to fill the void because we are uncomfortable with silence. I'd much rather stand in a quiet corner, sip water, and observe. People still came up to me and start talking. They don't want me to feel left out, regardless of the fact that I positioned myself on the parameter.

"You'd make more friends if you just take the initiative and talk to them," my mother said to me when I was nine.

"Leave her alone Patricia. Zoe doesn't like playing with the other kids. She'll make friends when she finds someone worth talking to." My father defended my quiet nature.

I take a long time to warm up to people. It took me a year to feel comfortable around Sylvia. The older I get, the more difficult it is to make friends. I accumulate acquaintances, but friends are few and scarce. Alison was my best friend when I was younger. We sat next to each other on the bus to school and in class. She'd come over after school and we'd sit at the dining table and do our homework together. We both had a crush on Warren Shaker. People thought we were sisters. They said we looked like each other. We both have beauty marks on our checks. Mine's on the left, next to my nose. Alison's was in the middle of her right check. We both have dark brown hairs, although Alison wore hers in a long straight pony tail, mine was in a short bob, just above my jaw line. We both wore eye glasses. We were inseparable, until the ninth grade. Her father got transferred to Portland. We talked on the phone and sent each other monthly letters. I selected my correspondence stationary with care. I liked Disney cartoon characters. But the days and miles got between us. We grow up and apart. She met Derek when she was a freshman at UNC. They married a year later. She dropped out of school to be a mother and housewife. We hardly talked by then. She was occupied with window treatments and onesies. I was busy with midterms and internships. I resented Alison for giving up on her dream of becoming a nurse, for giving in to Derek. Neither of us made an effort to keep the friendship going. Neither of us mourned when it died.

I looked up Alison on Facebook. She didn't have any privacy settings on her profile. I browsed her photographs freely. She has two boys. They resemble Alison, and are almost as tall as she is. Derek is the same, but Alison is different. She's matured. Her hair is lighter and perfectly coifed in a pixie cut. Her skin glowed with happiness and her eyes shun with pride as she stood next to her family. My heart congealed with envy. My eyes teared with a urning for similar love. My chest sunk with despair as I realized that I have missed the opportunity to be a young mother, to run around with my chidden, to go roller blading with them, to spend the night in a pillow fort and make shadow puppets against the glare of a flash light. I will never have that.

Is it selfish to have a child at my age, in my condition? Will my child suffer by having a mother in her forties? Will I be able to interact with the other mothers? What if they ban their children from playing with my son because I don't socialize with them? Of course it is selfish. I desire a child to give meaning to my hallow existence. Yet, what can I offer him in return?

I didn't friend Alison on Facebook. I return to her profile every once in a while and spy on her family through the photographs she shares.

\*\*\*

I have devised a routine. Routine is good. It gives structure to my day. I can plan around the stable activities. I wake up at 5:30. I do thirty minutes of yoga, mainly stretches. I shower and dress. I have breakfast, warm oatmeal, fruit and Greek yogurt. I sit at the kitchen counter. I read my books while at Starbucks for morning coffee and on the platform waiting for the train. I am currently reading *The Picture of Dorian Gray*. I keep myself busy at work. I break at 10:00 for a cup of green tea and 13:00 for Lunch. I have an apple at 15:00. I eat lunch at my desk to avoid congregating with others in the break room. I get home at 5:40. I change into my PJs and make dinner. I eat it in bed as I watch TV. I read a book and drink warm Chamomile tea. At 9:30 I get ready for bed. I perform my nightly beauty regimen. I exfoliate and apply night creme, rich with vitamin E. I apply moisturizer to my hands, elbows, feet, and legs. I put on thermal socks and go to bed.

Weekends are still haphazard. Sometimes I go into the city. I have an affinity for the Upper West Side. Other times I go shopping for winter clothes and household goods. I should work on devising a more rigorous Saturday and Sunday schedule. I allow myself extra hours of rest on weekends. I get up at six. I have breakfast at Starbuck or a Deli. I indulge in a doughnut. Saturdays are preserved for chores. I do my groceries shopping and laundry early in the day to avoid congestion and lines. I have discovered a farmer's market in Oceanside at the corner of Atlantic Avenue and Long Beach Road. I take the n15 bus and stop there on the way to Trader Joe's for organic produce. I clean the apartment. I changed the bed sheets and vacuum the rugs. I scrub the bathroom with bleach. I load the dishwasher and set it to Sanitize. I wipe down the stove and oven with disinfectant. I clean the refrigerator, throwing away expired products. I lysol the garbage bin, counter tops, and backsplash. I reward myself with Sushi for dinner.

\*\*\*

My mother called today. I was on my way home. I should have let it go to voice mail.

"Hi darling. How's everything? Have you settled in? Did you move any of your furniture from Chicago? Oh, of course not. You sold the condo furnished. Good God Zoe, you probably paid a fortune for new things, especially with prices in New York, not that Chicago was cheap, not like Charlotte. I'll pick up a few things and bring them over. That is, when you give me your address, of course."

My mother conducts unilateral conversations. My participation isn't necessary, I am, however, required to pay attention to what is being said as much so as to what is not being said, not that my mother is subtle with her passive aggression.

"Hello mother. How is dad?" I said, changing the subject.

"Enjoying his free time. I'm amazed how he's assimilated to retirement. He plays golf, all day, every day. To be honest, he is taking excellent care of the yard. He's started a small vegetable garden. He's in love with his tomatoes. Of course, you'd know all this if you visited more, or simply called every once in a while. Zoe, you do realize that I am the one who calls you."

"How's work?"

"Insane, nothing new there. Kids get ruder and dumber every year. I don't suppose that's very PC of me, but I'd have better luck teaching long division to monkeys. With all the technology available now, you'd think they be comfortable with numbers. Every year it's the same whining, *Why do I have to learn math? I can use my phone to calculate percentages, I'm not going to use math.* Don't they know that their phones, tablets and computers exists because of math. We have a new teacher, Evelyn. She's getting her master's in Education. She conducts her lessons in the playground. What does math have to do with swings and dirt? How can you solve equations without a board?"

My mother and I talk every day. At first, I thought she wanted to get an update on my life, a continuation of her dinner time interrogation. A ritual she started with my first day of kindergarten.

"Zoe darling, how was your day?" She asked as she served me chicken and mash potatoes.

I gave a detailed recollection of events. I was very thorough. As a child, I was excited about school and about learning. I liked the attention my mother bestowed upon me during those daily renditions. Yet, I soon realized that she was quick to criticize, not praise. Every A I accomplished, could have been an A+. I should have exerted more effort with athletics. Why wouldn't I go to the school dance, when all my friends were going to be there? Why wasn't I friends with Emily? I should have asked Alison to teach me some moves so I could've joined her on the drill team. I should have gotten contact lens because my glasses were a hindrance to my social life. It was foolish to be interested in computers, it should have been more of a hobby than profession. Medicine on the other hand was a career I could have sustained. I quickly learned to edit my responses and reverse the trajectory of the discussion.

"Zoe dear, how was your day?"

"Great. We started on trigonometry. How was your day, mother?"

I gave my mother the opportunity to discharge her negativity on her life instead of mine. It was her consolation. My father never gave much relief. When she'd complain about work, his response was always the same.

"You know that you don't have to work if it's making you unhappy. We don't need the money."

"Ken, I'm a school teacher. I don't make any money. Besides, who said I was unhappy. I just think the class schedule can be better managed."

"Then do something about it."

"Like what?"

"Take your suggestions to the vice principle. Volunteer to do it yourself. Complaining to me isn't going to solve the problem."

"I wasn't complaining. I was just telling you about my day."

"You're the one who wanted to work. You have to deal with the bad things to enjoy the benefits."

There are times when we simply need someone to listen to us and occasionally provide a shoulder to cry on. I was my mother's someone. Our tete-a-tete became an outlet for my mother's commentary on her life, a verbal journal. The discussion evolved to revolve around her day. I wasn't my mother's only victim, everyone was scrutinized. Yet, only I received her judgment. As her daughter, I was compelled to internalize her advice. She had my best interest at heart.

"I've had it with your aunt Linda. She asked me to go with her for a checkup. She was afraid her cancer might have returned. When Dr. Montgomery told her that she was still in remission, she ditched me to have drinks with her friends. She abandoned me at the hospital. I had to call your father to come and collect me because your aunt Linda drove us there. Can you believe that?"

"Why are you surprised? This isn't the first time Aunt Linda has done something like that. Have you forgotten about Atlantic City? You guys argued the entire weekend because she lost at Black Jack. She even called you her Bad Luck Charm."

"Well, that was different. She was upset for losing a lot of money. It was almost three hundred dollars."

"She's a mean bitch. I don't understand why you don't stand up to her."

"She's my older sister. You can't understand because you don't have any siblings. This is how sisters are."

At first, I was happy to deflect attention away from me. Yet, I wasn't spared her judgmental comments.

My earbuds were secured in place underneath my cap. My hands were firmly buried in my pockets. I walked down Park Avenue, blissfully ignoring my mother's rant. My mind retreated to a different destination. Standing at the intersection with Lincoln Avenue, I looked up at the flimsy fire escapes on the surrounding buildings, a harsh contrast to those of the Upper West Side near Columbia University. The fire escapes along Claremont Avenue were housed in blocks of cement, chiseled into Lily flower vines, perfectly harmonized with the neighboring architecture. They were an anomaly compared to most NYC buildings with decrepit steel ladders. Yet, those along Lincoln Avenue were exceptionally rickety. Stained with copper rust, they blended in with the bare brick backdrop. Apartment buildings in Rockville Center were three stores high, no taller than sixty-five feet. If a fire was to occur, it would be safer to jump from a window than chance it with the fire escape.

The light turned green and I crossed Lincoln Avenue. My mother's voice echoed in my ears.

"Are you still there Zoe?"

"Of course mother. Where will I go?"

\*\*\*

# March

A storm is expected to hit the east coast. Meteorologists predicted snow fall will start at 14:00. I'm working from home. I'm propped up in bed with my laptop. I'm surveying the sky for signs of first snow.

The TV is set to NBC's the Today show. Regular programing is interrupted with a storm watch, providing updates on the progression of snow towards the north. I called my parents yesterday to see how they were doing.

"We got a little dusting here in Charlotte. The storm hit further east." My father told me. "Stay warm and no driving until the snow clears. Do you hear me?"

"Dad, I'm almost forty. You don't have to worry about me so much."

"You'll always be my little girl, no matter how old you get."

My neck and back are cramped from sitting in bed all day. I stand up and stretch. I glance outside my bedroom window. It had started to snow. I was too occupied with work to notice. I walk over to the window and kneel by the sill for a better view of the cascading flakes. It's a few minutes past four, nightfall is near. The sidewalk and adjacent gardens are carpeted with a thin layer of snow. A blurred shade of green is visible below the icy coating. A smile erupts. The image evokes joyful memories of childhood. I picture snowball flights in the school yard and snow angels on the lawn. My mother used to pack me in layers of winter clothing, leaving only my eyes exposed to the weather. My father and I built snowmen. We'd christen them with names fitting their personalities. Toby was a civil engineer who was slender and short, with a hard hat. The Roberts snow family lived in our front yard for the majority of winter in 1989. It was exceedingly cold that season. It's been fifteen years since we last built a snowman together.

I stalk a falling snowflake until it delicately lands on the ground. I'm filled with a strong desire to go outside and have the snow perch on my arms and face. The wind diverges and picks up speed, hastening the dancing snow, forming slanting lines that are absolutely linear and only interrupted by passing vehicles. Drivers have turned on their head lights and are rushing home. The snow is getting denser, blurring the view into a white canvas. A hazy mist reflecting off street lamps is the only indication of snow falling. Small perfect flakes stick to the glass panels. Temperatures have dropped to freezing point, preserving the hexagonal prisms. I stare at the winter ornaments through the window and count eight peaks on each.

\*\*\*

It snowed all night. I looked out the window, heaps of fluffy snow covered the ground, rendering the suburban topology obsolete. Sidewalks, gardens and asphalt roads gelled into one massive white landscape. I was insulated in the apartment, sheltered from the cold outside. The uncleared roads mandated I work from home.

The snow hasn't melted. At nine o'clock, the porter cleaned the sidewalk with a power shovel, clearing a path between two snow embankments. It started to snow again at one.

I have no need to go outside, but I'm getting bored. Working from home is convenient. I get much more accomplished, being spared Melanie's interruptions. Yet, I have to remain logged on to the network for eight hours. I have completed all my tasks, so I play solitaire.

Two hours and thirty-eight minutes have crept by. I couldn't play solitaire any longer. I archived reports. I watched the virtual punch clock on my screen count down. One hour and twenty-two minutes left in the day. I checked Facebook and Twitter. Sixty-two minutes. I browsed news websites. Ten minutes. I was literally counting the minutes as snow continued to fall. I glanced outside at the canopy of white. I couldn't discern the outlines of the building across the street. A white film of thick snowflakes clung to the air.

It's eight o'clock at night. I'm getting ready to go to bed. My tedious job coupled with this snow sequester have pushed my mind to a brink of sanity. I clocked out at five and turnoff my laptop. An oval pinkish pattern developed on my thighs from the heat of the machine. I sat in bed, too bored to move, too restless to do anything. I was lethargic with the promise of spending all day in bed, that I skipped my daily yoga stretches. It was a long idle day. I could hear the virtual tick tock of time slowly passing. Boredom burrowed in my bones and chased away all interests. Nothing entertained me. No books. No movies. No TV. I spent the day in a void of nothingness. I simply sat in bed, waiting for the day to end. We spend our entire lives in waiting for something or someone. As children we can't wait to grow up, only to long for childhood as adults. In school, we wait to graduate. We wait to be employed. We wait to fall in love. We wait to have children, then we wait for them to grow up, go to school, graduate, and fall in love. Our lives is an endless spiral of waiting.

The nothingness has ushered in melancholy. Darkness prevails within. How can I spend eternity waiting, not knowing if it'll happen or not? How can I go about my life normally, hoping that the waiting ends tomorrow, only to start over again.

\*\*\*

Uniform pop pop pop sounds emit from the pipes running the length of the walls, warming the room. The floor boards next to my bed creek as I get up and walk to the bathroom. I look at myself in the mirror. "Who are you?" I ask. I wash my tear-stained face. I look at the soapy water swirl down the drain with a gurgle. The aging apartment is akin of an ailing body. They both require regular maintenance to function properly. You have to tinker with the plumbing and electricity to stop the lights from flickering and keep the toilet flushing. Both need a coat of paint to stay appealing. Memories lurk in very corner. People say, "It has character." But no one wants to inhabit the haggard home. People say, "They don't make them like they used to." But no one wants the old, the used, the tired. We water the lawn and clean the gutters, just to keep up appearances, while the inside is moldy and infested. I'm filled with debris. I creak. I crack. I pain. I ache. I stand demolished. I turn to dust.

\*\*\*

I haven't left the apartment in five days. I wake up every morning at five and linger in bed. I force myself up and make coffee. I eat breakfast while standing at the kitchen sink, staring at the fire escape and parking lot below. Everything is covered in snow. I go back to bed.

The storm was severe on the northern states. The office is closed for the rest of the week. I clock in at nine o'clock and check e-mails. I stay in bed. I don't bother changing out of my pajamas. I work. I read. I watch TV. I am too listless to shower or cook. I joined an online video streaming service. I watch back-to-back episodes of TV shows I was too busy to watch before. Hours slowly bleed into days.

Snow has finally stopped falling. Last night, I heard the snow plow clearing the roads. I peeked out of the window this morning, and the sidewalk outside my building had a clear path. I couldn't stay confined indoors any longer. I tucked my skinny jeans into rubber boots and put on my heavy jacket. I ventured to the grocery store to buy milk.

I stepped out of the building with a smile. A gust of frigid air hit my face. I pulled the zipper of my coat as far up as it would go and I put on my grey mittens. Tall mounds of snow lined the sidewalk. They came up to my mid-thigh, completely engulfing the fire hydrant. Roads were cleared overnight, yet a fresh coating of snow covered the asphalt. Frozen clusters of snow were melting. Puddles of dirty slush pooled at street corners. Icicles glistened in the shimmering sun. Streets were deserted.

I walked the length of the pavement adjacent to my building. The porter did a good job in clearing the snow. He even cleared the entrance to the parking lot and sprinkled it with salt. I naively assumed that all sidewalks would be similarly safe to walk on. As I moved north on Park Avenue, the clear pathway disintegrated into a slippery snowy carpet. The top layer of snow had melted overnight. As the temperatures fell it solidified into ice. I was confident that my boots would hold up in these conditions. I was adamant to stay outside as long as I could. It took me fifteen minutes to carefully tread across the one block to Lincoln Avenue. I climbed over a mountain of plowed snow to press the cross button on the traffic light. As I steady my stance against the light post, a slab of iced shattered at my feet. I waited for the light to turn.

I was happy to be outside, despite the cold, despite the wind, despite the ice. I crossed Lincoln Avenue and continued west. I followed in the footsteps of past pedestrians. I placed my boots on their preserved footprints, reading the names of various labels embossed in reverse on the soles of their shoes to guarantee a readable imprint. They were a billboard of footsteps. I slipped as snow accumulated on the heels of my boots.

I finally reached Village Avenue. My face was drenched in sweat. My heart thumbed in my chest with the strain of the walk. I stretched my arms outwards to balance my steps, overworking my core muscles to remain upright. As I approached the corner, I lost my footing and collapsed, landing violently on my knees. The instant I realized that I was going to fall down, I reached out and held on to a dilapidated red pole outside the dilapidated CD shop. I pulled myself forward. Kneeling before the mercy of the weather, I gave up on my dairy quest and limped back home. "This is why you drive. So on days like this, you can get milk without throwing out your back." I told myself. I felt a bruise spreading under my jeans. I cautiously hobbled along, smirking at a woman who gingerly sprinted into the Yoga studio ahead.

***

When I was looking at apartments, the realtor said the one on South Park was in a prime location, a few blocks away from the train station and city center. A line of bars and restaurants extended from front street across the train station, all the way down South Park, a block away from my apartment. There are three Sushi and Hibachi restaurants, two Thai places, five pizzerias, four generic bars, an Italian restaurant, three steakhouses, a Starbucks, two ice creme parlors, and six delis.

I'm not much of a bar person. I don't drink. I find bars crowded and noisy. The food is often greasy stomach lining to allow further alcohol consumption. Eating alone at restaurants is intimidating. I prefer take out. I call in my order while at work, right before leaving, and pick it up on my way home. More than often, I pop into a delicatessen for readymade meals. Park Avenue Deli have the best potato salad and veggie burgers.

The week after the storm, I passed by the deli every day and picked up dinner. I got the same thing every evening, a cherry soda, two bags of chips, a pound of potato salad, and half a pound of tuna veggie salad. This was my comfort food. One evening, I saw an old lady sitting by herself at the table nearest the door, eating a sandwich. She was reading a book, *Beautiful Ruins*. I had seen her before on the train. She's in her fifties. Her hair is cropped short and completely white. She wears khaki trousers and brown hiking boots. She carries a backpack, but never hunches under its weight. She wears unusual caps. The first time I saw her, she was wearing a cap with red, yellow, orange, and pink strips, with a red pompom on the crown and red braided ribbons from the ear flaps. We both exited at Rockville Center station. She walked ahead of me down Park Avenue. Our courses separated at Lincoln Avenue, where she turned left. I saw her a couple of times in

King Kullen and around the neighborhood. There she was, all alone, eating dinner and reading a book. *That's me in twenty years*, I thought.

What will happen to this woman when she's gone? Will anyone mourn her death? Will anyone be at a loss? Probably not. What will happen when I die? My parents will be sad, but their lives will proceed as normal. Will anyone visit my grave? What if I get hit by a car? Will my dead body rotten in the morgue with no one to claim it? What would happen if I were to disappear and leave behind no trace of my existence. Will my parents convince themselves that I was a fantasy, that they dreamed me up? I'd leave no void, no emptiness. I will absolve the space I consume in the universe for someone else more worthy, someone who will leave a mark on the world, someone who will be missed when they are gone.

I don't want to be the old lady.

\*\*\*

It was a clear day. I walked around, exploring Rockville Centre. I bought a crumb cake from a little bakery in front of the train station. I ventured up Village Avenue passing a Dunkin Doughnuts, a coffee shop, dry cleaners, hair stylists and acupuncture. They were housed in a single-story building near Saint Agnes Cathedral. The landscape was Devine, even in midst of winter. The grass shun with pride of a lawn that was loved and well maintained. Tall pine trees surrounded the main structures, full ferned branches bounced in the breeze. Congregation members hurried across the parking lot to attend Sunday mass.

The image relayed into single family homes, a small office building and an abandoned gas station sheltering battered cars and rusty sail boats. Across a small intersection was a strip mall with a liquor store, a chain pharmacy and Home Goods. The parking lot was vacant. Beige shopping carts queued next to the entrance. The automatic doors swung open as I stepped forward. The seemingly small structure contained endless arrays of furnishes, linen, throw pillows, decorative mirrors, glassware, stemware, stoneware, baking supplies, gourmet condiments, shower curtains, pots and pans, and dishes. The merchandize stretched in never ending aisles.

I circled the store once, to compose my excitement. I picked up items that caught my eye and placed them in a shopping basket. I accumulated wealth, realizing with each step how little possessions I had with me in New York. I bought agave honey and cheesy popcorn for 5.99. I paid 9.99 for two non-stick skillets and 2.99 for a silicon spatula. I would have bought a dozen decorative pillows had I had a couch. I would have bought a tan leather arm chair, had I had a car to transport it. I happily carried my bounty in the store's branded shopping bags. I resolved to go back latter for a set of nesting table I had my eye on.

I returned to the store several times. I stocked up on cooking utensils. I restrained my purchases to only one item per trip. I don't need much. Although, I did buy two hand blown ice creme bowls. They are clear aqua green with turquoise spirals.

I haven't been using the kitchen much. I sustain on microwave dinners and takeout. My vigor for cooking retuned with the allure of new pots and pans. They taunted me. They wanted to be utilized. I made pancakes for breakfast. I baked brownies for the office. I made a lentil casserole and blue berry cheese cake for dinner. The extra calories added much needed motivation to exercise. I joined a health club.

\*\*\*

I was awakened by a scream. I was frightened, not sure if I was dreaming. I sat up in bed, still confused. I checked the alarm clock. It was eleven thirty. My eyes squinted in the dimly lit room. My ears were alert to all surrounding sounds. I heard it again, a loud shriek, that of a woman in agony. It was the couple next door. They were having an argument.

They are always fighting. I hear them shout at each other through the wafer-thin walls. The female howls with a shrilling voice, the male answers in muted subdued murmurs. I fight the urge to press my ear against the wall to hear what they are saying. The quiet of my solitary domesticity is regularly interrupted with loud thuds as they bang doors with such force the walls shutter and the floor boards creak. The building deliberately reminds me that I am surrounded by people. We endure humanity's duality, through our senses. We hear the beauty in a child's laugh and the ugliness of adultery. When I first moved in, I'd retreat to the living room to spare myself the specifics of their arguments. I wonder why none of the other tenants complain, or am I the only one to hear them? Maybe they, too, are listening. Maybe they, too, are ashamed to be listening.

Sleep escaped my eyes. I was prying on their privacy as I sat in bed, attentive to their argument, waiting for it to be over. I flipped through TV channels. I propped my head on the upright pillow and watched a British show on PBS about World War II. I glanced at the alarm clock, it was almost two. They've been quiet for a while now. I wonder if they are done fighting. At least they have something worth fighting for. What do I have?

I can't go back to sleep. I close my eyes and focus on the mundane, willing my mind to be still. It won't abide. The TV is set to the Weather Channel. Inches of rain, slippery conditions, decreased visibility, words as such echo in the room. I focus on the weather. My lids grow heavy. My mind drifts to images of rain, snow, and wind. I'm trapped in a building. I frantically run through corridors, looking for an exit. Every door opens to a wall of foamy snow. Wind gusts slam them shut. My eyes fling open. My heart races with anxiety. I change the channel in search of a more soothing atmosphere. Sitcoms erupt with false laughter. Horror films amplify with menacing scores. Click. Click. Click. Program after program flicks on the screen. I find solace in the shopping channel, in the repetitiveness of exhibitions, the countdown of inventory, and the background noise of nighttime purchases. My mind is void of thoughts, is void of dreams. The memory of my neighbors' fight hangs over my head like a halo. Their silence blesses my sleep.

***

# April

I filed my taxes today. I usually do them as soon as I get my W-2 form, but I wasn't organized or well planned this year. April reminded of the impending dead line. I use an online application for convince. My W-2 is automatically uploaded to the website and data from previous years is archived for easy retrieval. Completing the questions and scrolling through all the screen is a bit time consuming. So, I dedicate an entire day to the process.

I started immediately after breakfast. I keep a soft copy of receipts and important documents on my laptop and a backup drive. I retain hardcopies in a folder labelled with the relevant year. These are filed in a disaster proof box. I collected all related documents, both hard and soft. I fanned them out on the bed in order of usage, mirroring the sequence of questions. My Macbook rests on my lap with the power cable snaking from its magnetic port to the electricity outlet under the bedside table. I set out to do my taxes for last year.

The lack of student loans and presence of a steady mortgage simplifies the process. It keeps it consistent. I log in with my username and password, click on W-2 and watch the screen summarize the year in numbers, defining me in a string of integers, FED ID and SSA. These digits tell the story of my employment history and contribution to society, both federal and state, both taxes and benefits. I examine the numbers every year. Like a spinning taxi meter, they measure how far I have gone. Even when life stagnates, the meter still counts. The questions that pop up on screen are an annual reminder that I have achieved nothing. I simply accumulate wealth, move to a higher tax bracket. Unchanged marital status. Lack of dependents. Minuscule Medical bills. My life is at a halt, a standstill. The government is not satisfied with my anguish over no husband, no children, no family. It penalizes me further with extra taxes. No deductions for a single debt free person.

It's two o'clock. I've completed e-filing my taxes. I opted for the deluxe charge, a premium to guarantee tax audit support. I shut my laptop and look around. "I really should buy some furniture. I'm not going to spend the fucking year on this bed." I said out loud.

I purchased furniture online. I have never been keen on shopping. Department stores overwhelm me. I tend to frequent small shops and boutiques. I know what I like and I know where to get it, while wasting as little time as possible. My casual wardrobe comes from The Gap. My business suites are from Banana Republic. Shopping conjures up memories of following my mother around the mall as she chased a trail of sale signs. We'd spend an entire weekend looking for new shoes. Every year I'd select a pair of hazelnut Hush Puppy loafers. Yet, every year my mother would insist on taking me to all the department stores and have me try on all sorts of shoes. She'd kneel down and press her thumb against the tip of the right shoe to gauge the fit.

"Just walk in them a bit. See how they feel," she'd say.

I obliged but declined to give in to her bargain finds. Hush Puppies were comfortable and durable. Loafers paired nicely with jeans, trousers, and skirts. Why did I have to waste an afternoon searching for something new, when my good old Hush Puppies would have sufficed?

"You need to step outside your comfort zones. Try something new." My mother replied. "Why don't you try on these Keds. Laura, Jan's daughter, she wears her Keds with short socks. She looks adorable in them. What about LA Gear High-tops? Doris says they're all the rage."

My mother was relentless, and so was I. She believed shopping was a sport all women should willingly engage in and thoroughly enjoy mastering. It was our opportunity to bond. But shopping was exasperating and physically daunting. Carrying mother's shopping bags from store to store. Holding heaps of clothes as she tried them on. Forced to give my opinion.

"Honestly, Zoe, you're such a grouch. I drove all the way to Southland Mall so you can spend the entire time moping. You need to pop your head out of a book every once in a while and act your own age. Live a little. Have a bit of fun."

"I enjoy reading."

"You need a balance. Reading and learning at school is fine. But you also need to go outside and hang out with friends. Do things other girls do. Why don't I make an appointment with Marcy. We can get our hair done together, or get a mani pedi."

"Mom, I can't type with manicured nails."

\*\*\*

There were two poppy seed bagels rolling down South Park this morning. Another one laid neglected by the curb. Someone placed their breakfast on the roof of the car and drove off. The two bagels twirled around themselves then came to a rest on the pavement. One faced upwards on the east side of the road, the other faced downwards on the west side. I smiled at the scene. I waited at the intersection of Lincoln and Park. The sun shun in my eyes. I took out my sunglasses and placed them on my face. Spring is finally here.

I surveyed the area. Trees which stood bared just yesterday, blossomed and fluttered in the cool breeze. A man dressed in a dark suit, skateboarded towards Sunrise Highway. He flung his dry cleaning over his shoulder. A couple of bicycles appeared east and west Merrick Road. Beaming exposed faces adorned the sidewalks, pale from hiding behind scarfs and caps all winter. Coats and boots remained present, yet most people discarded gloves. "Enjoy the weather," said Anne as she handed me my Tall Pike Place in a Grande cup.

I sat on the platform, sipping coffee and waiting for the train to arrive. I faced south, overlooking the east bound tracks. I felt faint sun rays on my back as I sat on the cold metal bench. Seagulls perched on the peaked slanted roof of the movie theater. The morning crowd grew. A few exposed maroon nails peeked out of open toed sandals. Chatter from waiting commuters echoed in the background. I opened *The Grapes of Wrath* and commenced reading. I frequently looked up from the lines for prose, distracted by the festivities of oncoming warmth.

Arriving at Freeport, I decided to walk to work. I stopped at Dunkin Doughnuts and bought a variety box for the office. I turned left at Walgreens on the corner of Merrick and Church Street, and continued east towards the rising sun. The path was familiar. I see it every morning behind the protective glass of the bus window. The air was crisp, yet a bit cold against my face. I walked past boxed stores, some opened for business and others still closed. To my left was Quiznos and Pep Boys. On the right was a hairdresser and tile merchants. Although still early in the day, Merrick was busy with traffic in both directions. Further east, I waited for a light to turn. I crossed a narrow side road and glanced over the inclined drive through. It was a Home Depot parking lot. Some trucks and station wagons occupied the space. Along the chain fence stood bands of men, day workers, hoping for a job. They were scattered in discrete groups, comrades, united in the struggle to support their families. Their faces beamed with smiles as they greeted new comers to their pack, oblivious to the fact that job chances decreased with each addition. Maybe they are just optimistic. Maybe they realize that they can only wait in the parking lot and hope for a leaking pipe or a house in need of painting. Brooding over unknown possibilities is fruitless. We all wait for chances. They either come or disappear. These simple men have figured out what corporate executives neglect to realize. We spend hours scheming and back stabbing for business opportunities. We tire, day and night, to gain nothing in return. We make a good living and own nice things, but we pay the price with our health, our sanity, our emotions.

I arrived at the office sweaty and invigorated from the walk. My mood was lighter. I put the box of doughnuts in the break room, next to the coffee machine. All morning long, people walked up to my desk and thanked me for the sugary treat. "A clever way to get to know everyone. I'm sure they appreciate the gesture," Charles said, with a mouthful of chocolate glazed doughnut.

\*\*\*

I enjoy the walk home in the warm weather. I leisurely prance down Park Avenue. Yesterday, a man exiting the UPS store along Sunrise was carrying a clear plastic bag of packing peanuts. He put it down to open the trunk of his car and it fell open releasing white foamy particles. They danced in the wind as the man franticly tried to recuse the bag.

I sit on a bench outside the senior center. The magnolia tree has sprouted new buds. The aroma trails in the air. Bars and restaurants open glass partitions and extend their dining rooms to the sidewalk. I listen to the buzz of the surrounding shops from the solitude of my bench. Tree branches bounce in the breeze, waving at passing traffic, alluring us into enjoying the warm spring weather. A tall Japanese Fir overshadows the building across the street. Long branches protrude perpendicular to the ground like the hands of a vagabond begging for sunshine. They extend away from the building, shading the sidewalk. The branches on the other side have been sawed off. I naively thought they diminished on their own in an act of urban obedience. But nature can't be tamed, just broken.

\*\*\*

I had a rough night. At three fifteen the fire alarm outside my front door went off. My eyes darted open upon hearing the first dongs of the alarm. I instinctively jumped out of bed and pulled on a pair of jeans over my pajamas. I reach for a small disaster proof box with important belongs, and ran down stairs. The lobby was empty. I looked outside through the glass door. I didn't see any flashing lights nor heard any sirens. Was this a dream? I continued to hear the alarm. Yet, none of the other residents rushed to the lobby.

Walking up the stairs, the faint long beep became more prominent with each step. On the third floor, I stood glaring at the fire alarm next to the staircase door. It let out long beeps followed by a brief period of silence, signaling that the batteries needed to be changed.

Adrenaline pumped in my veins. The constant sound of the alarm chased away sleep. I laid in bed and stared at the ceiling. Why did I jump to save myself from the fire? Is natural instinct stronger than our will?

Eight years ago, I wondered aimlessly in life. I wasn't unhappy per se, but I wasn't happy either. Work didn't motivate me, yet I continued to go every day. I'd smile and reply, "Great," when asked how I was doing. I wasn't great. I was done with life. I had achieved everything I set out to achieve. There was nothing left for me to do. I was lonely. Sylvia was married and lived in Washington. I'd go to movies and concerts alone. I'd dine alone. I'd sit on my couch alone. I'd cry alone. I had nothing left in my life to be passionate about. I read books to pass time. I lost myself in fictional stories. I lived vicariously through fictional characters. Faulkner and Tennessee Williams saved me from the darkness lurking in my mind. I read Wordsworth in the morning and carried the verse with me all day. I'd dreamt of Lord Benedick and Beatrice. I was content. I had a resolve to live in waiting for hours spent with my books. I researched the human body. I learned to nourish my organs and exercise my muscles to lift the aftermath of the darkness. It remained, buried deep. It resurfaced at times. I'd despond for a weekend and climb out of the abyss on the lines of Virginia Wolfe. I had a system for dealing with the darkness. I learned to live with it. Although I was done, I didn't have the courage to let go. I pondered death for months. I eliminated options that didn't guarantee definite results. I prolonged my suffering in search for the perfect plan, with no pain, no hesitation, no chance to change my mind. I never acted on these notions, yet

I found comfort in knowing I had a choice. I found the will to live a life I no longer valued.

Yet, when faced with the opportunity to give in and let go, my natural instinct was to survive. Are we programmed to save ourselves when faced with danger? Years of fire drills have trained our muscle memory to react in a certain way. Our instinct to survive is intrinsic. We have no control over it.

\*\*\*

It's been raining for the last two days, washing away buds that bloomed at the first hint of warmth. Shallow lakes of rain water have formed in the pivots of street corners. White translucent blossoms of crab apple trees float on the surface, reminiscent of a wedding precession. Hard rubber tires of passing cars do not hesitate before crushing the delicate petals and splashing pedestrians with stagnate gutter water.

Lighting and thunder saturate the clouds. Temperatures dropped as swiftly as my hope for spring dispersed. The walk to and from the train station is an aquatic adventure. Moisture and cold penetrate multitude of clothes and attack my bones. My black rubber Hunter boots slouch through puddles. I balance my backpack by extending both arms sideways like a clumsy tightrope walker. Pot holes in the street fill with water. They freeze overnight into dangerous black ice. Withering magnolias litter green patches of grass. Daggers of rain pelted from the sky, tear apart tulips and daffodils. Brown petals cover pathways, duplicating the gloom of darken skies above. Flowers will blossom again. Nature is resilient like that. It's torn down, only to rise again.

\*\*\*

I took the train into Manhattan one evening after work. I emerged from Penn station at Thirty Third street. It was dark outside. People were rushing. I continued south east until Madison Avenue. Tall skyscrapers boxed in the surrounding bars and pubs. Employees, on their way home, made pitstops in Flatiron for an afterwork drink. The area was inhospitable to solo patrons. I felt unwelcomed, out of place. There was a small cafe next to the Gershwin Hotel, Birch Coffee. A few round metal tables with two chairs each congregated around a coffee bar. I ordered a cappuccino and biscotti. It was raining outside. I dunked the biscotti into the frothy elixir and watched the early evening traffic.

This weekend, I went up to the Upper West Side for Lincoln Center's Independent Film Festival. I ventured around Broadway, early Saturday. Shops were closed. Long lines formed for toasted bagels. I took my Tall Pike to Verdi Square next to the Seventy Second Street subway station. An elderly couple was out for a morning walk. The woman was dress in a blue Channel suit with a black bowler bag hanging from the crock of her elbow. Her free arm was hooked in that of a gentleman in a tweed sports jacket. They walked in silence. He slowed his pace to match hers. They were both content with each other's silent company.

My favorite place in Manhattan is Bryant Park. They have taken down the ice rink and surrounding structure, exposing the sun hungry lawn and the back of New York's Public Library. I go there at eight o'clock in the morning. I walk along Sixth Avenue. I get an Earl Grey tea from Pret A Manger and croissant from Le Pain Quotidien. I cross Fortieth street and walk up the cobblestone steps. I select a seat near enough to the carousal that I can hear the French lullabies and children playing, but far enough that their voices don't distract me. I face the tall buildings. Sun rays streak between the branches of London Pane trees. I sit there and read. I write in my journal. I watch the children play, wondering if I'd be a better mother to a boy or girl. Do parents connect with their children because of biological bond? Will I connect with my child? Will my DNA compel me to love her? I am not constantly fond of myself, why would I love someone who is half mine? How can I love my child, unconditionally and expect the same from him in return? Do all parents have these doubts? Should ask Mother? Perhaps Sylvia?

"Being a single parent isn't easy. You can't take a vacation from being a parent and you can't change your mind after they arrive. If you're not fully committed to being a parent, you'll end up resenting your child. You'll both be miserable."

"What'll happen when you meet someone? Finding a goodman is difficult as it is, even more so for single mothers. How will he feel about raising someone else's child?"

"Will you go to a sperm bank or ask someone you know for a donation? Who? Will he be involved in the child's life? How will you explain his absence to the kid when he grows up?"

"Adoption isn't easy, especially with your traveling schedule. You are going back to consultancy? How else can you afford a child? Trust me, they cost a fortune."

Too many questions I don't want to address. If I'm going to do this on my own, then I have to reach a decision on my own.

I miss Sylvia.

\*\*\*

"Hi. It's Zoe."

"Oh my God. Where have you been? I sent you over a dozen e-mails."

"I know. I've been busy with everything."

"Are you all settled in?"

"Yes. I've been in the apartment since February."

"That was quick."

"I had a good realtor."

"How's the new job?"

"Good. Everyone's really nice."

"Nice."

"How are the kids?"

"Crazy. Are you happy?"

"Yes. Why?"

"You don't sound happy."

"Just tired."

"Do you need anything?"

"I'm okay."

"Oh, by the way Adel is trying to get in touch with you. He called me last month. He wasn't sure if he had the correct e-mail because he wrote a few times but you haven't replied."

"I haven't been checking my Hotmail on regular bases. Do you know what he wants?"

"He wasn't specific. He just said that he wanted to talk to you about some research work."

"I'll call him."

"Maybe I can come over next weekend. We can see show and have dinner, or something."

"I don't know. Maybe later."

"Okay. Don't be a stranger."

"Bye."

"Bye."

After hanging up with Sylvia, I called Adel.

"Adel," he answered.

"Hi, this is Zoe."

"Finally. What on earth are you doing in New York?"

I've known Adel for three years. We met at a conference in Florida and have been friends and research colleagues since. I answered his question truthfully. It was a relief to unburden my thoughts to him. I told him everything I wanted to reveal to Sylvia, but couldn't. He was an astute listener. He gave me room to express myself without interrupting.

"You have a lot to contemplate. Do you think it's a good idea to isolate yourself? I understand that you're trying to make a rational decision, nevertheless emotions will factor in. A new city and job, no family or friends. This was very bold of you. But it seems unnecessary."

"Maybe it is. It felt right. I needed a change. I need to clear my head so I can examine the situation from every angle."

"I suppose you know best, and I suppose you're not available to come to Boston."

"I'm sorry, Adel. I'm just not up to research at the moment."

***

# May

The weather is getting warmer. I leave the window slightly cracked open at night. They haven't turned off the heat in the building. I come home to find the apartment stale after baking in the heat all day. I wake up in the middle of the night drenched in sweat. However, Park Avenue keeps me awake. White noise from the TV doesn't draw out the shouts and screams of bar patrons along North Park. They vividly trail to my bedroom window on the third floor. The disruption worsens on Friday evenings. Party fueled weekends shake the quiet serenity of the city to its core. Long Islanders ride to Rockville Centre for the weekend bar scene. On Saturday mornings, a concourse of discarded pizza boxes, beer cans and splatters of vomit litter the sidewalks leading to the train station. Sunday mornings, families queue outside of deli's and bagel shops for breakfast. Children's laughter echoes in Starbucks as they accompany their parents' coffee fix. For the most part Rockville Centre is a quiet domestic dwelling, but not on Friday nights.

    I get as much as sunlight as I can. I eat breakfast in the kitchen, facing the fire escape. It isn't much of a view, but the sun shines through the kitchen window. Cooking for one is disheartening. I make small meals, but there's always leftovers. I eat half the batch of pancakes and keep the rest in the freezer.

    I spent the weekend at Home Goods. I made a few trips. I couldn't carry everything all at once. A lady recommended I commandeer a shopping cart to transport the goods home, but I couldn't bring myself to do it. The thought of me pushing a shopping cart around Rockville Center was too sad. A warm breeze brought about the first signs of summer. I happily hugged the creme colored plastic bags filled with merchandize as I walked down Center Avenue. I made separate trips to bring back a small folding oak table and a bench with a parrot embroidered on the seat. I placed them in the hall way next to the entrance, below a rectangular mirror with a decorative faux wooden frame. I sit on the bench to put on my shoes, and the table houses a small mail caddy and ceramic dish where I keep my keys. I put a coat rack next to the door. It carries my scarves, hats, and umbrellas. I got place mates and a center piece for the dining table. To the right of the couch is a six-cubby bookcase. To the left is a round silver table with a side lamp. A long narrow bench sits in the middle of the area rug, separating the couch and my new forty-seven-inch TV. I use it as a coffee table. Next to the living room windows stands a plastic folding table I use as a desk. I got it from the hardware store on Sunrise. It's similar to two large ones in the laundry room. I covered it with a pale grayish blue table cloth. It has large yellow, green, a purple flower stitched in wool. When I sit in my wicker desk chair, I look out at South Park from the window to my left. I spent the majority of the weekend furnishing the apartment. Sunday night, I ate leftover dinner from the week before at my dining table and sat on the couch watching TV with a cup of coffee and a scope of vanilla ice creme.

\*\*\*

Returning home to an empty house is desolate. I was too busy in Chicago to notice. But here, the emptiness is palpable. Voices from the TV set is the only sound to arise out of my apartment. I never turn it off.

"Wouldn't it be nice to have someone waiting for us when we get home? Someone who'd be genuinely happy to see us." I once asked Sylvia during a flight from San Antonio.

"Get a dog," she replied.

I have considered a pet, a nice little Yorkie. If I am to pick up someone else's poop, feed and bathe them, I demand absolute affection in return. But, locking a dog in an apartment all day by itself and abandoning it for weeks while on business trips, didn't seem like a fair trade.

I walk by a flower shop every day. It's next to the train station. They have orchids of every color on display. The bouncing buds caught my attention. I stood at the entrance, enchanted by the dancing hues of summer. I bought a white moth orchid with flecks of pink. Two tall stalks stood proudly in a terra cotta pot, supported by invisible stakes and rhizome clips. Each stalk held eight jubilant flowers. The shop assistant placed the pot in a small cardboard box for easy transportation. She loosely wrapped the plant in clear cellophane to shield it from the wind. I placed it on the window sill of the bedroom window. It watches over me as I sleep.

\*\*\*

It's been a long weekend. I haven't done much. No, that's not true. I haven't done anything, actually. I've been in bed since Friday night, staring at the TV, following nothing in particular, and crying. The tears won't stop. My loneliness is suffocating. I grasp for breaths as I'm further submerged in an ocean of solitude. I cradle my knees in a synthetic huge. I allow myself to sob in hope that it might be cathartic, but it's not. I should at least do one load of laundry but I can't convince my body to move. My back and limbs ache. I rest in bed, thinking it's beneficial. I must be coming down with something. I have only eaten crackers and cheese for the last two days. I don't even have the energy to order food.

I wear my tears proudly. But, I simply wish they'd stop. People think crying is a show of cowardliness. It takes courage to be sad. Yet, we cry when we're happy too. I suppose the warmth of our own tears is comforting. The saltiness cascading down our lips reminds us that we are alive. We always seek the company of others when we are emotional. In happiness, we are overtaken with a desire to spread the joy. In sadness, we find comfort in loved ones. Happiness and sadness mar us in the same way. We carry them both within. New happiness congers up memories of past happiness. The same with sadness, yet happiness is more fleeting. It evaporates quicker from our souls. It is easily replaced by sorrow. My heart swells with agony. It crushes my lungs and suffocates my voice. It weighs heavy on my limbs. It fogs my mind. When it lifts, it leaves behind a mist of despair that hangs inside me, anticipating the next wave of melancholy.

I crawled out of bed Sunday afternoon and went for walk. Signs of summer were everywhere. Daffodils and tulips have sprouted new buds. Leaves fully conceal branches that were bare less than a month ago. Nature is a continuous cycle of renewal. It encompasses ends with beginnings, death within birth, laughter within tears. The skies rain, only for the sun to shine brighter the next day. Winds blow away magnolias, spreading their fragrance in the air. Fall foliage sully the grass and fertilize the soil. Darkness passes to light. Hope breeds misery. We break our hearts because we hold on the notion of happiness, of betterment. If only we could relinquish all hope and accept our lives as they are, we'd avoid anguish. But our hearts are not rational organs. They have to be broken beyond repair, beyond reproach, to give up on happiness. But we never learn. 'This too shall pass' and 'If it doesn't break you, it makes you stronger' numbs our senses. We should confront hope before it infiltrates our expectations. That is true strength.

Emptiness leads me to despair. I must try to keep busy, to devise a weekend structure to distract me from my thoughts.

\*\*\*

It was Memorial Day. Everyone in the office was excited about the long weekend. They all had plans to visit family or go into the city. Those who could, took Friday off to get an early start to their vacation. Those who couldn't, came into work. I planned every minute of the seventy-two hours to avert the idleness, to avoid meandering into the follies of my mind.

We've been blessed with beautiful weather. Green algae like fungus coats tree trunks, complimenting the green overtures of the leaves. Short shorts have reprised their place in the wardrobes of teen girls and some teen hopeful women. Exposed pale legs flip flop on the sidewalks. The roads are congested with convertible sports cars. I was keen on completing all my chores Saturday and Sunday, saving Monday for the ocean.

Long Beach is twenty-five minutes away by bus. Monday morning, I had breakfast, then packed sunblock, a brimmed hat and a book. I walked out of the lobby and crossed the street to wait for the 10:07 n15 bus to Long Beach. I sat to the driver's right, next to the window. The narrow side streets of residential Rockville Centre, lined with single story homes in gentle whites, blues, and greens, gave way to the wide lanes of Long Beach Road. It strung together an endless array of fast-food eateries, chain stores, wireless carriers, and grocery shops juxtaposed against a peppering of independent Mom and Pop businesses. Sad looking buildings clamped together in strip malls, indifferent to their existence like faceless strangers. Today a McDonald's, tomorrow a Bank of America, the day after white washed with a 'For Sale' sign. The city's incinerator loomed in the background, occupying empty land and emitting white cloudy smoke from tall chimneys.

The bus ride was short, but slow. Summer was upon us. Everyone spent that Monday morning stuck in traffic and incased in their air-conditioned cars, en route to the ocean. The bus finally arrived at Long Beach, passing by Island Park, with its curvy streets, shopping plazas, and fisherman's wharf houses. Yet another Park Avenue stretched parallel to the shore, separated by single level buildings of delis, restaurants, and ice creme parlors. The salty atmosphere had weathered external layers of paint and store signs faded from the sun. I exited at the last stop, next to the LIRR station. A narrow azure glistening strip peek-a-booed between the rows of stucco beach houses. The boardwalk and ocean beckoned me. They drew me in as the tide did the sand.

The skies were clear. The sun shun brightly. I climbed a wooden inclination to the boardwalk. A few beach goers lounged on the sand. A lone parasailer bobbed up and down, trying and failing at lift off. The water was too cold to entice a crowd. Yet, some swimmers did brave the frigid ocean. The waves were too timid to tempt surfers. Families remained on the boardwalk. Children on tricycles peddled on the stretch of wood. Their parent followed closely behind. Adjacent balconies overlooking the ocean, loitered with ladies basting in the sun. I walked to an empty bench and sat down. I took in the serenity of the waves. I inhaled the scent of the ocean. I watched the tide eat away sand and wash it into the water, eroding the shore. The very same waves hit coastal rocks, clusters of sand clinging together, building strength from one another, hardening with each wave slamming against them, breaking those waves into foamy froth.

I took off my leather thongs and walked down to the beach. My feet sank in the packed sand. The dense white grains, cool under the surface, crept between my toes as I approached the edge of the shore. Despite the busy boardwalk, the beach was a quiet retreat. I sat on the sand with my palms buried under the surface. My legs arched before me. My feet landed at the damp surface of lapping water. Sun rays escaped through the seams in the brim of my straw hat, sprinkling my face with warmth. The ocean stretched out to an infinite drop. The blue tones intensified as the water extended into the horizon. I was overwhelmed with a strong desire to continue walking, to be swept away by the tide.

\*\*\*

I have enrolled in a few classes at NYU to combat loneliness. I have creative writing on Mondays and Wednesdays, from seven to nine, conversational French on Thursdays and film critic on Fridays. Creative writing is in a building on Forty Second Street. I sit at the large window overlooking Bryant Park for inspiration. I keep to myself during breaks and share as little as possible. I'm lonely but I don't crave human interaction. I simply want to be around other people.

Tara from creative writing invited the eight of us from class to attend a discussion on the effects of Victorian Literature on modern notions of romance. She was moderating the event and wanted the reassurance of familiar faces. It was held at an independent bookstore in Upper Manhattan, near Columbia University. I skipped conversational French and took the One train uptown. A wooden cart stood on the sidewalk next the entrance. It held an assortment of used books. I entered the intimate show room, cased in floor to ceiling bookshelves. To the left was a children's section, stacked with primary colored miniature furniture and displays. To the right was a large table covered with columns of discounted books, catering to the literary requirements of Columbia students. I picked up a copy of *Milton's Paradise Lost*. I flipped through the pages of the heavy paperback. The smell of glue and ink seduced me.

"I'm here for the discussion on Victorian Literature." I told the shop assistant.

"It's in the loft upstairs." She pointed to the end of the store and said, "The stairs are right next to the notice board."

I did as instructed and walked up the narrow staircase. The loft stood bare, with clean walls and large windows overlooking Amsterdam. A long leather couch stood next to the wall. Two sections of wooden folding chairs were stacked in a make shift auditorium. I sat down on a chair in the last row of the section nearest to the exit to facilitate a quiet escape if the evening got too boring. I took off my jacket and draped it over my knees. I started on Paradise Lost.

The space filled with mainly college students. A few people from class waved at me as they filed by. The AV coordinator tested audio equipment with the usual thump thump thump on the microphone. He mounted digital cameras on tripods and placed them in appropriate vantage points.

The panel consisted of graduate students. The discussion was courteous, if uninspiring. Similar insights could be found in a Huffington blog post. Panel members nodded in agreement and waited for their turn to comment. They invited audience members to participate. Some people walked to the microphone stand and annunciated their questions, taking the opportunity to stealthy mention their personal opinions. The allotted sixty minutes passed by swiftly. I was keen to get back to Adam and Eve and the Devil. I collected my things and walked to the podium to thank Tara for the invitation. As I reached the landing at the end of staircase, I saw that the notice board was replenished with posts. A freshly printed paper stood out – Research Assistant needed. Students welcomed. I photographed the contact information with my phone and left.

\*\*\*

# June

Work and classes keep me busy during the week. But on weekends, I'm left to my thoughts. I enjoy my solitude, not having to unnecessarily interact with other human beings. Yet, my mind won't stay still. The image of swaying legs occupies my dreams. It soothes me to sleep and remains with me throughout the night. Other images do not fight away insomnia, even that of a sleeping baby. I saw my arms cradle her. I felt her warmth radiate against my chest. I smiled at the image. Then, my mind interjected with doubt. My heart raced with fear. I returned to the other image to calm me.

I need a weekend hideaway, a retreat from my thoughts. Something to occupy my mind and tire my body. I called the phone number and inquired about the research assistance position. I had an appointment for an interview.

I took the LIRR after work. I was meeting Oliver Scott in his office at Columbia. I hate Penn station at night, packed with after work traffic. I hate it even more so on Friday evenings. The crowds multiple with each step. I exited the platform near Seventh Avenue and walked the length of the station towards Eighth, to take the One train uptown. The crowd was overwhelming. They towered over my 5' 2" frame. I was claustrophobic. I bent my head upwards to breathe uninterrupted. The tide of people carried me as I gravitated towards the subway station by sheer momentum. I clenched my Metro Card in hand to avoid any delays at the turnstiles. I skipped a few congested trains until one arrived with ample standing room. I stepped into the car and took off my back pack. The bulk of the bag aggravates other passengers. They collide into it as they exit the train, forcing my body in the counter direction. I placed the bag on my feet to avoid contact with the subway floor. One hand firmly clutched the metal railing to steady my stance, the other held on to the back pack's handle.

I exited at Hundred and Sixteenth Street. I stopped at Starbucks for a coffee and quick snack. I ate a chocolate chip cookie and I navigated the streets towards Philosophy Hall in the Morningside Heights campus on Amsterdam. I lingered outside to finish my coffee. I walked up four floors to office 402 and knocked.

"Come in," replied a voice.

I opened the door and walked in. The room was saturated with a strong scent of cigarettes and vanilla. A small desk stood to the left of the door and a coat rack to the right. I waited in the doorway to be admitted. A man leaned against the desk, facing a lone window. His back was to me. He looked over his shoulder and gestured for me to enter. I took off my jacket, sat down, and placed it over my knees. I surveyed the office. Photographs covered every available space on the wall. I couldn't find the man in any of them. The space was well organized. Neatly stacked volumes resided in a short bookcase in front of the desk. A sage utility jacket suspended from a dry cleaner's hanger on one of the hooks of the coat rack, next to a motorcycle helmet. A pair of black rimmed glasses rested on top of my resume in the middle of the desk. A three-tier wire tray was on the left. Sheafs of documents cluttered the remaining surface.

I sat uncomfortably in the chair and waited for the man, Oliver Scott I presumed, to finish his conversation. He walked over to the desk chair. Wedged between his should and ear was a cellphone. He silently mouthed "I'm sorry," as he rummaged through the papers on the desk. He was six feet tall. Light ice-tea strands of hair curled over his forehead. He brushed the caramel locks away with his long fingers. He spoke with a British accent. His narrow almond eyes were a light shade of grey with small pupils. His irises were perfectly outlined with a dark diameter. His cheeks sat high on his long face. He had a healthy pale complexion and powder pink lips.

I realized that I was staring. I looked away and occupied myself with the buttons on my jacket.

"Sorry about that," he finally said. "I'm Oliver, and you must be Zoe."

"Yes."

"Right. So, you'd like to do some research work?"

I didn't answer.

"Well, Zoe. I've gone over your cv. You're a project coordinator?"

"Yes."

"And you live on Long Island?"

"Yes."

"You studied Computer Science, a while ago?"

"Yes."

"And now you want to be my research assistant."

I silently stared at him.

He swiveled his chair slightly to the left, crossed his legs, and pursed his lips. He glanced up at me and said, "Well, frankly Zoe, I'm a bit perplexed. I must admit that I googled your name. Up until recently, you were a prominent technical consultant in Chicago, with extensive research in," he put on his glasses and consulted my resume, "Big Data." He enunciated every letter. "So, you left all that to come to New York to be a project coordinator?"

"I needed a change."

"Ah. Yes. Yes, I can empathize. I, too, needed a change. But, I'm not brave enough to embrace such a radicle change as you did. I simply substituted York University for Columbia. I'm a visiting lecturer."

"Yes, I know. I, too, googled your name."

He smiled in response.

"So, tell me Zoe, why do you want to be my research assistant?"

"To keep busy during the weekends."

"You do know that my field of study is English Literature?"

"Yes. It came up in the google search."

"Of course. So what does Big Data have to do with Dickens?"

"Big Data infiltrates every aspect of our lives. However, research is research. You're looking for someone to review documentation, examine studies, transcribe, and proofread your work. It's the same, regardless of discipline."

"I suppose that's true."

"It's categorically true. Research Methodologies are the same."

"You feel very strongly about your opinions."

"Because I am right."

"Well, I have some more meetings before I decide. Thank you for coming. It was interesting."

We stood up and shook hands over the desk.

\*\*\*

The weather is very warm. I feel guilty about turning on the A/C, but it's getting too hot at night. I wake up drowning in sweat. I keep a water bottle on the night stand and frequently take sips. Nevertheless, I wake up in the morning with a dry mouth, chapped lips, and scratchy throat.

I spent the weekend at Bed, Bath and Beyond examining fans, comparing the pros and cons of each option. I selected a model small enough to easily carry on the bus. I keep it under the window unit to circulate the cold air. It doesn't oscillate. I pivot it upwards so it can disperse cold air emitting from the A/C. On cooler nights, it sits comfortably on the unit's wide wooden enclosure just below the window sill. I open the glass panel high enough to expose the fan's circular head to the open breeze. The fan's constant humming masks the outside sounds, complimenting the monotony of the Shopping Channel, awarding me cool restful nights.

\*\*\*

"Oh, hello. This is Oliver Scott."

"This is Zoe Baldwin."

"Of course. I assumed it would be you to answer the phone."

"I thought I'd confirm that assumption."

"Right. Right. Well, anyway. I'd be happy to have you as my research assistant."

"When do you need me to start?"

"I know the flyer said weekends. Could you possibly pass by during the week so we could discuss tasks and requirements."

"I could come in after work. When?"

"Right. How about tomorrow?"

"Fine. At your office?"

"Yes."

"I'll be there at 6:30."

"Great. Great."

"Okay. Looking forward to it."

I hung up.

\*\*\*

"Hi. Thank you for coming in." Oliver greeted me.

"No problem." I replied.

He smiled.

"Did you come directly from work?"

"Yes."

"Why don't we pop out for a bit of food. We can talk over dinner."

"Fine."

He jumped out of his chair and slapped his hands together. "Great, let me get my jacket." he said.

I waited in the doorway. He walked over to the coat rack and lifted the sage utility jacket from the hanger. He threw it over his right shoulder, simultaneously shimmying both arms into the sleeves. The jacket gracefully fell onto his frame, in the most ostentation display of dressing, like a super hero flinging on his cape. I must have been staring because he glared at me and asked, "What's the matter?"

"Nothing. Let's go." I mumbled as I surveyed my shoes.

Oliver led the way to a nearby vegetarian restaurant. He lit a cigarette the moment we stepped off campus. I walked a few steps behind to avoid the foul smoke. He crossed Broadway and walked in a doorway. The host greeted us with a wide smile.

"Professor Scott, how nice to see you this evening."

"Oh, Geoffrey, please. I've been coming here almost every night. You can just call me professor." He smiled.

Geoffrey tucked two menus under his arm and guided us through a maze of dinners. He seated us in a private section in the back of the restaurant. The area was dimly lit, with candles and sheltered spot lights. Five narrowly separated square tables, big enough for two, were aligned against a long burgundy banquette. Oliver waited until I wedged myself in before occupying the opposite chair.

"Would you like to start with something to drink?" asked Geoffrey.

"Yes, please. I'll have my usual. Zoe?"

"Sparkling water," I replied.

"So one gin tonic and a sparkling water. Your waiter will be right over to take your order. Enjoy your meal." Geoffrey left, masterfully threading his way back to the front of house.

Oliver looked at me with a closed lip smile. He brushed his hair back with his fingers and said, "God, I wish I could smoke indoors. Do you know that I can't even smoke in my fucking flat, excuse my language. I'm subletting from a mate who's on a sabbatical in Sweden. Before letting me have the place, he insisted that I only smoke in the bathroom, with the window opened, because, and this is a direct quote, he doesn't want cigarette odor to permeate the upholstery and walls. Unbelievable. In the dead cold of winter I had to stand in the loo, blowing smoke out of a fucking window. Unbelievable."

"At least you were indoors."

"That's true. Hope you don't mind vegetarian food. The cuisine is fusion and very innovative and they have the best bartender in Up Town. He pairs cocktails to your food."

"I don't drink."

"Of course."

"You wanted to discuss tasks?"

"Yes, right. Let's first order. Have you decided what you want? I'd be more than happy to make a recommendation. If you don't fancy anything on the menu, I can ask them, to put something together to your liking."

I ordered a deconstructed taco. Olive had a sushi platter. We talked about his work. He's working on a book about Feminism in Renaissance Literature. "Sofie, my editor, suggested I hire a research assistant to get things moving along. I'm a bit behind schedule. I'll need you to transcribe notes, cross check references, and help out with other duties as such," he said. "I promise to mention you in the Thank You section," he joked.

"That won't be necessary. You'll pay me for my services. Why do you want me to come in on weekend? I can do this work from home," I asked.

"Weekends are dedicated to the book. I'd like you to come in early and keep me on track. Having you there will keep me honest and away from distractions. Sofie expects the first draft by late September."

"Fine."

We agreed.

\*\*\*

My orchid is still alive. I diligently follow the care instructions that came with it. I keep it in my bedroom overnight and in the bathroom during the daytime, away from the heat. Every morning, I press my finger in the soil to make sure that it's moist. Two buds have sprouted new blossoms. They gradually opened up over the weeks.

This weekend was my first as Oliver's assistant. He'd prefer I called him professor, but I don't. I call him Oliver. He calls me Zoe.

I took the 6:30 AM train to Penn station. The LIRR Babylon line runs parallel to Sunrise highway. The view from the train is the same regardless of direction. Every town you pass has the mandatory iHop, Dunkin Donuts, and local dinner named after the town. They all sit prominently on the highway. Car dealerships and clusters of one-story buildings housing independent shops alongside big-name stores like Radio Shack fill empty spaces. There's the random pop of warehouse structures of Home Depot and grocery stores. All the towns looked alike, the only distinction is the post sign on LIRR stations announcing Merrick, Freeport, Rockville Centre, and Lynbrook. On the brink of Queens, Sunrise and LIRR part paths. The train continues on to the back yards of single-family homes leading to St. Alban, until it relays to the transportation hub at Jamaica station. There, trains align on parallel platforms, synchronizing arrivals and departures for connecting schedules. The station is adorned with the high line of JFK's AirTrain, shuttling travelers to the airport. Further west, seven story red brick apartment buildings of Kew Gardens, the Tudors of Forrest Hill, and graffiti littered under passes surround the train tracks. Manhattan's skyline greets us as we enter the tunnel leading to Penn. Traversing rails, utilized and abandoned train cars, stacks of rusted steel, and blackened wood beams lay strewed in the yards before the tunnel, next to metal sheets and power mega plugs. An industrial image ushering the train away from suburbia and into a commercial paradise of skyscrapers.

I often occupy seats facing the opposite direction. Not that I prefer them, but they are usually available. Watching the scenery in reverse is like rewinding a video reel and bidding the vista farewell. The train this morning was vacant and my seat faced west. I welcomed the steel structures that stood astute in the horizon as the train headed into the city.

I was standing in front of Oliver's door at 8:07 am. I was late and I'm never late. I always arrive a few minutes before schedule. This being Saturday morning, it would have been rude to arrive early. I lingered along Broadway, breathing in the Upper West Side. I gently knocked on the door. I heard stomping sounds. A faint 'coming' escaped through the closed door. My arms ached from carrying a paper bag of bagels and accompanying paraphernalia. I waited.

I heard locks unhinge and chains unlash. The door squeaked open. He was still drowsy with sleep. Caramel ringlets of hair cascaded over his brow. His narrow eyes were mere slits. His voice hung low and heavy with snooze.

"You said eight o'clock," I apologized.

"I know," he replied.

"It's seven past eight."

"Come in Zoe."

His plaid pajama bottoms hung loosely on his body. His ass was disappointingly flat. His stark pale feet thumped on a Persian rug in the hallway leading to the kitchen. His feet were huge. They stretched out on the red and blue silk tapestry like a duck's foot. The bones connecting the toes to his ankle visibly stood out against his paper white skin.

"I brought bagels," I said.

"Ah, sustenance. Good girl." He smiled, "The toaster's over there. Coffee mugs are in the cupboard above the sink. Here's the cutlery." He pointed and directed me to various location in the kitchen. "Coffee beans in the freezer and French press is next to the kettle. If you don't mind making a pot of coffee, while I jump into the shower." He left.

I familiarized myself with the kitchen and made the coffee. He set up a place for me to work next to his desk, a sad plastic table and dining chair. Our respective desks faced one another and overlooked Seventieth Street. I sat at my working space and waited. He emerged, twenty minutes later, dewy and freshly shaven. He smelled of menthol and grapefruit.

"I see you've found your desk. Let's start with some proofreading." He gave me a stack of documents to revise.

"What will you be doing?" I inquired.

"I beg your pardon."

"You need me to help you stick to a schedule. So, what do you aim to accomplish today?"

"Right. Right. Well, I'm working on a chapter draft."

"Which chapter?"

"Eight. Chapter eight."

I wrote 'Finish Chapter Eight' on a legal pad and placed it on the working space between us.

"What else?" I asked.

"Beg your pardon?"

"What else needs doing? It's Saturday, should you be doing laundry?"

"I don't do laundry on Saturdays."

"There's nothing else you should complete today?"

"Finishing the draft will suffice."

"Finishing the chapter will suffice." I corrected.

"Yes, ma'am. But first I need a cigarette."

For the rest of day, I proofread and he worked on the chapter.

\*\*\*

I flew to Toronto today. As a project coordinator, I'm not required to travel, but Charles wanted me to meet the Toronto team. During the interview, I was adamant that I don't want to travel. I was exhausted after years as a consultant with weekly airport visits and bands of non-descriptive hotel rooms. This is my break, an opportunity to recompose myself. If I am to move forward with a child, I will have to minimize traveling and possibly eliminate it entirely for the first few years.

Charles apologized profusely for sending me to Toronto.

"I'm really sorry about this Zoe. You said you don't want to fly around and all. It's only an hour from La Guardia. It'll be like going into the city for a quick meeting. At least there won't be any traffic in the air."

I had no other option but to agree. Charles politely apologized, yet he made it clear that I was going to go to Toronto. The flight was fifty-seven minutes. However, the cab ride from La Guardia to Rockville Centre was seventy-five minutes long. I got home at four thirty. As I walked up the stairs and rummaged for my keys, I murmured 'Home Sweet Home.' After every business trip, when I'd get back to Chicago, I'd say the same thing as I slid the key into the lock and turned. I paused, astound at my proclamation 'Home'. Was New York my home now? Was the apartment my home? What constitutes a home? The brick and mortar, the furniture, or the memories? How can you tell if memories are a recollection of actual events or simply fantasies conjured to entertain a lonely mind, when you have no one to authenticate them. Maybe a family makes a home. So, is Charlotte my home? Am I destined to have no other home until I have a family of my own?

My mind mulled over this thought as I walked into the apartment, automatically dropping my keys into the ceramic dish. I walked to the bedroom and discarded my clothes. I showered and dined. I was so familiar with my surroundings, I simply went through the motions with ease. Maybe familiarity makes a home, and thus offices become more of a home than our residential dwellings, and our colleagues become our family.

It's dark outside. I've prepared my uniform for tomorrow and packed my lunch. As I was applying night creme, I looked into the reflection of my eyes. I no longer see a stranger, but a familiar face. It's not a face from the past, but someone new. Someone I'm just getting to know. Maybe a home is the place where we find ourselves after being lost. We never stay the same. We're constantly changing, and our home evolves along the journey of discovery. With every new person we become, we find a new home, be it our family, work, a book, or even a favorite park bench. It's the place where we go to be ourselves, unadulterated, unmasked, pure, and simple us.

***

# July

I've been waking up at four. I don't need much sleep. Six hours seems sufficient. I use the extra hours in the morning to transcribe notes. The tedious task has proven adept in filling the void. My mind is silent. Oliver's breathless voice dictates notes into the microphone of his earbuds as he cycles up Broadway. He later uploads the file to a shared folder where I access it. I transcribe the notes the next morning and upload the document to the same folder for his revision. It is a perfect system. Yet, he insists on compiling chapters by hand. I work on these notes during the weekend while he edits and revises. The research work is quite mundane, yet I am determined to do my best. English literature doesn't seem that difficult. I suppose this is an unfair assessment. All research is arduous. I had an illusion that literature research used lucid artistic prose, similar to that being examined. Literature research is not literature. It's an abundance of quotes in essay form, not prose. It is logical, concise, and insightful.

Oliver's revisions are challenging. He uses a purple felt-tip pen for edits. It is difficult to decipher his scribbles. I haven't gotten used to his handwriting. Last weekend, I was making some changes to the manuscript when he asked, "Could you show a bit of enthusiasm while working?"

"No," I replied.

"Would paying you more help?" he asked jokingly.

I peered over the rim of my glasses. My right eyebrow instinctively arched and my lips pursed.

"Right. Sorry for that." He retreated.

I'm happy with the momentum of the recorded notes. I have completed a significant amount of work during the week and rewarded myself by taking the weekend off to thoroughly clean my bathroom and kitchen. Early Saturday morning, I scrubbed the toilet, sink and tub with bleach. I cleansed the drains with a mixture of baking soda and vinegar. I cleared the medicine cabinet and the cupboard underneath the sink. By 10:45 am, I had finished the bathroom. My phone rang. I took off my mask and rubber gloves to answer. It was Oliver.

"Yes?" I asked.

"Hi, it's Oliver. May I come over?"

"What? No. Why?"

"Please Zoe. The apartment upstairs is moving in, or out. I don't know which, and I don't care. I can't get anything done with the hammering and drilling. Please let me come over."

"No. Go to a coffee shop or something."

"Too distracting. Please."

"It's Saturday."

"'Yes, and you're supposed to be working. I was kind enough to let you have the morning off."

"Yes and I have shit to do."

"I won't bother you. I promise. I'll just sit in the corner and work, quietly. Please."

"Fine."

I gave him direction to Rockville Centre. Two hours later, I heard a knock at the door. I answered in my protective gear. I pulled the mask off my face. It rested on my chin.

"What on earth are you doing?" He asked.

"Sanitizing the kitchen and bathroom."

"And hence the strong smell of Chlorine."

"It's bleach."

"May I come in?"

"Oh, yeah. Sure." I moved aside and held the door open. He timidly walked in and looked around.

"Have you just moved in?" He asked.

"No, I've been here a few months."

"Waiting for the rest of your furniture to arrive from Chicago?"

"I've cleared my desk. You can work from there."

I continued with my cleaning ritual. I cleaned the fridge and loaded the pots and pains in the dishwasher and set it to sanitize. Oliver worked quietly all day. He occasionally stood up, laced his fingers behind his head and flexed. He'd stand for a few minutes, staring out of the window.

At six, I set the table and called him over. We dined on baked tilapia and mushroom risotto.

"That was really good. Thank you," he said.

"You sound surprised. You didn't think I could cook."

"No. I'm amazed that you spent the day 'sanitizing,'" he used air quotes, "and then you made dinner."

"It was nothing."

He helped clear the table. He loaded the dishwasher as I made coffee and scooped vanilla ice creme over warm brownies. It was nice to dine with someone. It was nice to hear someone compliment my cooking. It was nice to chit chat with someone about the weather and holiday plans. It was nice to argue with someone over the Bronte sisters.

He settled back at the desk. I kept to my bedroom. At ten I asked, "When are you leaving?"

"Oh, fuck. Sorry, I didn't realize it was so late. I don't suppose I can spend the night?"

"No."

"I'm in the middle of something. I won't be able to pick-up the pace, if I leave now. You won't even know I'm here."

"You're insane."

"Yes, that's the general consensus."

"Fine," I said.

\*\*\*

Oliver was sleeping on my couch. His shoes and socks were neatly lined against the wall. His jacket was hanging on the back of the wicker desk chair. His long arm dangled over the side of the couch, grazing the chocolate brown rug. He still had his reading glasses on. I debated removing them, but decided to leave them as they were. I quietly went about my morning, trying not to disrupt his sleep. I snook out for the paper and I returned to the scent of freshly brewed coffee. He inquisitively looked over the stove as I walked in.

"I thought you were asleep," he said.

"I was getting the Times. What are you doing?"

"Making breakfast. It's the least I could do to thank you for accommodating me last night."

"I brought bagels."

"I'll take those. You can sit down at the table and wait to be served."

He placed a plate of scrambled eggs, a sliced toasted bagel with cream cheese, and mixed berries in front of me. He sat down in the opposite seat with a similar dish. We ate in silence. I sipped coffee and he drank orange juice.

"Ah, she smiles."

I hadn't realized that I was in fact smiling.

"This was very kind of you," I said. "There are clean towels and individual toiletries in the hallway closet next to the bathroom. You can wear my robe while I wash your clothes."

"Miss Baldwin, are you suggesting that I need a shower?"

"Yes." I said as I collected the dishes.

At four thirty, he got up from his affirmed position at the desk and said, "We're going out." We walked up Park Avenue to Press 195 for a late lunch. The weather was sunny and warm. He selected a table near the opened glass panels.

"So, why would a hotshot consultant leave her job and abandon her research to come to New York and be a project coordinator?" He asked.

"I needed a break. I'm trying to figure out what to do with my life."

"Oh, please. You've probably had a series of five-year strategic plans since you were a toddler."

"I had a plan, but I'm not sure if it's really what I want to do. I need to clear my mind and make some decisions."

"So, this is temporary."

"Maybe."

\*\*\*

Oliver texted last night. He asked me to meet him at Union Square. We agreed to meet in front of Barnes and Noble. I arrived early to browse for books. By the time we met at eleven, a heavy shopping bag encumbered my movement. My neck stiffened from carrying it around.

"That's a lot of books. Why don't you buy them online?" Oliver asked when he saw my purchase.

"I didn't intend to buy so much. It just happened. When I see a book I like, I must have it. I can't wait twenty-four hours to have it delivered. I immediately want to flip through the pages and read it. Immediately, no waiting."

"Ah. So, Barnes & Nobel to you is what Barney's is to other women. Instead of shoes, you gorge on books."

"I can buy shoes, too. One doesn't negate the other. What are we doing here?"

"Shopping."

"Shopping?"

"Yes. I packed the bare essentials. I need more summer cloths."

"Okay, and what am I doing here?"

"Helping."

"Oliver."

"I'm color blind. I need someone to help me pair things together, and a woman's opinion never hurts."

"Am I the only woman you know in New York?"

"You're the only one available on a Saturday morning." He said with a no offense smile.

"Why did we have to come here to shop? Manhattan is full of stores."

"You don't like this neighborhood?"

"It's not that I don't like it. Surrounded by skinny tall people makes me feel very inadequate. I feel like a hobbit, more Bilbo Baggins than Frodo. Everybody's walking around with a purpose, like they have somewhere important to be. Hello, it's Saturday morning, you don't need to power walk to brunch." My voice was a few pitches too high and my hands flew about with animated gestures.

"I'm sorry. I didn't know you felt this strongly about um, here. I was told that there are amazing restaurants. I thought we could have lunch together."

I wouldn't say that Oliver has bad taste, it's more bland than bad. He favors chinos and jeans, monochromatic shirts with white tees, and loafers. Oliver frequents The Gap and Uni Quo. Mike, on the other hand, would be appalled to pass in front of a Gap or Uni Quo. Why am I thinking of Mike? Juxtaposed against Oliver, he seems fictional, imagined off the pages of GQ. I suppose Mike appreciated opulence over substance. Just because Oliver shops at The Gap doesn't make him more genuine than Mike.

It was a tiring day. I don't enjoy shopping. I'd rather spend the afternoon at the theater. Oliver bought slim shorts in every hue. We paired these with pastel cotton shirts and vibrant t-shirts. He got a driver cap and straw fedora. Plagued with our purchases, we hobbled to Prince Street for lunch at a quaint bistro. I collapsed in the metal seat and quenched my thirst on freshly squeezed lemonade. We sat in silence, examining the menu. I glanced up and saw a woman standing on the sidewalk waiting to cross the street. She was wearing a grey jersey minidress. There were no silhouette lines associated with under garments. Her pale complexion was daunting against the ghostly fabric. Her long legs extended down to a pair of plain flip-flops. The light turned. She was busy on her phone and sprinted across the street.

"Look at her, with her tight ass and little jersey dress. There's not a jiggle in her wiggle. Not one. I hate her so much," I said.

Oliver looked at the woman and said, "You do know, men prefer jiggly women."

"Are you fucking kidding me?"

"No, I'm being quite sincere."

"Oh my god. You need to be quiet now."

"Why? Are you penalizing me for being honest?"

"Yes. There's a time for honesty and a time for either lying or saying nothing. Jiggly women? Honestly? Well, here's a question for you, do men find boobage sexy?"

"Boobage?"

"Yes. When a woman with a large cleavage wears a bra two sizes too small and her boobs protrude over her décolletage forming a spillage of boobs, boobage."

"I can't believe you just said that." He laughed.

"Come on, answer. Since you're being quite sincere."

"Well, I suppose it depends on the boobs." He pressed his lips in chagrin, "Yes, men do like breast. We'll look at them, if the opportunity presents its self. It's actually a compliment."

"Really? Having nice boobs is not an accomplishment. There's nothing we can do, short of surgery, to have perky bouncy breasts. Now, a firm butt, that we work for, and abs and chiseled arms. I remember in my twenties it didn't matter if I worked out or not, or gorged on pizza. I never gained weight. Something changes around thirty. If you give in, only once, and have a tiny burger. It remains permanently lodged on your hips. Every time you squeeze into a pair of jeans, you are reminded of that rogue burger and the extra ten pounds that you can't lose regardless of endless hours at the gym. As you get older, you justify the flashing numbers on the bathroom scale by the myth that muscle weighs more than fat. You're convinced that retailers are conspiring against you, altering their garments so you fit in a size twelve rather than an eight. But we all know, it' that damn burger you scarfed down ten years ago."

"I guess you'll be having the salad then."

Oliver gallantly refused to split the check. He hailed a taxi and gave me a lift. He dropped me off at Penn station. He pressed his lips to my right hand and said, "Madam, thank you for a very entertaining day."

We parted ways.

\*\*\*

The temperature was in the eighties today. The humidity was intolerable. I exited the Seventy Second Street subway station at eight thirty. Buildings shaded the sidewalk as morning dog walkers pranced down Broadway. I looked up at the sky, a mixture of clear blues greeted my gaze. I smiled as I raised a Starbucks paper cup to my lips and drank the remaining sips of coffee.

Oliver opened the door in his navy dressing gown. He didn't sleep well. Dark crescents appeared under his eyes. He offered no greeting as I walked in. He turned his back to me and continued with a phone conversation.

"Yes, mother, it's very thoughtful of you to call me on my birthday. Thank you."

It was his birthday.

"No, I'm not irritated, just sleepy. I was asleep, you know… It's not even nine… No, I wasn't out late last night. Even if I were, I would have been celebrating my birthday. Don't I have the right to celebrate with friends… No, mother, I'm not over exerting myself partying in New York with chippies."

I stood in the foyer and eavesdropped.

"I'd love to have you and dad over. Maybe around Christmas?" He turned around and glared at me, surprised by my presence. "Mom, I have to go… I love you too." He hung up.

"Good morning Zoe."

"Good morning Oliver."

I set about my regular routine. I positioned myself at the desk and transcribed the week's notes. I typed through a jumble of notebooks, iPhone notes, scrapes of random paper, and voice recordings. Hearing Oliver's voice directly broadcasted into my ears felt like he was roaming inside my head.

Oliver showered and shaved. He changed into kaki cargo shorts and a navy polo-shirt. He combed his wet locks away from his eyes with his fingers. He sat across me, at his desk. I glanced up at him between sentences and asked, "What best describes you, immediate gratification or delayed satisfaction?"

He was annoyed with the distraction. He took off his glasses and rubbed his eyes, "What?" he asked.

"What best describes you."

"Yes. Yes. I heard you the first time. Why are you asking?"

"Just answer."

"Some context please."

"Immediate gratification or delayed satisfaction?"

"Delayed satisfaction," he answered with a sigh.

Oliver worked at his desk. He occasionally glanced out of the window. I hide in the kitchen for the rest day, out of his way, preparing dinner. He, too, was oblivious to my presence, or he simply ignored me. I roasted a small chicken and steamed vegetables. Dessert was a Banoffee pie. One afternoon, we passed by a Haagen Daz. He was very excited to find Banoffee flavor.

"Every Sunday, we'd go to my grandmother's for dinner. She made a Banoffee Pie for dessert. I later discovered she bought it from Tesco. But it didn't matter, it's still my favorite. It's the perfect combination of textures and flavors." He said between mouthfuls of ice creme, beaming with a radiate smile.

I laid the table. He walked over and asked, "This is what you've been doing all day?"

"I made dinner. If you are good and eat all your vegetables, dessert is a surprise."

"What's the occasion?"

"Your birthday."

"No, my birthday was last Thursday."

"Better late than never. Sit down and eat."

When we were done, I brought out the pie. His beaming smile reemerged. I lit a candle and put it in the middle of the whipped creme topping. I placed it before him.

"Make I wish."

"Does it sound too conceited to say that I already have everything I could wish for."

"No, just blessed."

He blew out the candle and took a huge spoonful. He said, "Delicious. Absolutely delicious."

"Delayed satisfaction."

"Ah, what would I have gotten if I said immediate gratification?"

"A Banoffee pie inspired dessert."

He furrowed his brow inquisitively.

"Bananas, vanilla ice creme and toffee sauce."

We ate the pie out of the pan. I loaded the dishwasher before leaving. At the door, Oliver helped me into my rain coat. He kissed me on the check and said, "Thank you Zoe for a wonderful birthday."

\*\*\*

I woke up Tuesday with an aching body. My nose was congested. My stomach was unsettled. I had influenza. I had too many tasks to mope around home. I crawled out of bed and went to work. I took two Ibuprofen pills to quench the pain.

My fevered spiked midday. I hydrated with fruit juice and sports drinks from the vending machine, causing multiple bathroom visits. Every time I was on the toilet, someone would walk in to use other stall. It was the same person every time. She'd click clack in her brown pumps, lock the stall, flush the toilet, pull out a toilet seat cover, tinkle, flush, wash her hands and leave as rapidly as she peed.

My symptom fully manifested by the end of the day. Before leaving, I passed by Charles to let him know that I wouldn't be coming in tomorrow. He told me to take the rest of the week off.

I passed by CVS for flu medication, nasal spray, effervescent vitamin C, vitamin water, crackers and canned soup. I stocked as many juice bottled as I could carry. I was too tired to eat when I got home. I took off my shoes and climbed into bed with my uniform still on. I slept.

I woke up in the middle of the night. I forced my body out of bed. I changed into pajamas. It was one thirty. The apartment was pitch dark. I turned on the bedside lamp. I had no appetite for food. I took some of the medication and went back to bed.

I wasn't any better the next day. My head was fuzzy. I was nauseated. I forgot how many pills I had taken and when I had last taken them. I ate some soup. I couldn't distinguish the flavor. My congested nose compromised my taste buds. I crushed saltine cracker in the soup to settle my stomach. I placed a bottle of vitamin water on the bedside table and went back to bed.

My fever didn't subside. I looked up a General Practitioner within walking distance of the apartment and made an appointment. The doctor ordered me to rest and prescribed antibiotics. I laboriously walked home and crawled into bed. I was jolted awake by a ringing phone, three hours later. It was Oliver.

"Zoe, hi. I was going to leave you a voice message. I need you to pass by Friday evening and pickup my notes. I'm going to the Hampton's with friends this weekend. I still need you to transcribe the notes, though."

"I'm sorry but I'm really sick. I don't think I can come over." My voice was a whisper. It was painful to talk.

"You sound awful."

"Yes, well apparently I have a nasty bug."

"Apparently? So, you've been to the doctors?"

"Yes, I have just gotten back. I need to pick up my prescription, but he told me to rest. I don't think I can make it into the city on Friday."

"Of course not. Go back to bed and focus on getting better."

\*\*\*

Dehydrated from the fever, I reached for the water bottle on the nightstand. It was empty. As I sat up, the room started to spin. I closed my eyes and clutched the sheets. I sled my legs off the bed. I sat there for a moment to regain my balance. Still dazed yet confident that I could stand, I got out of bed and walked to the bathroom. I stood at the sink, staring at the mirror. My eyes were sunken in the hallow of my skull with dark circles underneath covering half my face. My complexion glistened with perspiration. "My God, you look awful," I whisper to the reflection. I leaned over the sink and splashed my face with cold water, trying to wash away the ugly. Bile rose up my throat. I paused to make sure I wasn't going to throw up, before exiting to the hallway. I braced myself as I embarked on the journey to the kitchen to replenish my water supply, leaning against the wall as each step threatened my balance. I finally reached the living space. In the glow of the muted TV I saw Oliver's silhouette. I couldn't believe he was still there, hunched on the sofa, asleep.

I stood in disbelief, thankful to him. Thankful that he came bearing soup. Thankful that he picked up my prescription. Thankful that he stayed. I walked forward and gazed down at his still body with his legs angled in a V formation, right arm tucked under his head, glasses teetering on the brink of his nose, and mouth ajar. I smiled while securing his reading glasses off his face. I removed various pillows wedged between his body and the upholstered cushions, trying to give his six-foot frame additional room. I pulled the throw off the ottoman and covered him. I unlaced his shoes and removed them, wondering if there's any truth about the proportion of a man's foot size and his penis. I placed a pillow under his head, releasing his arm. My fingers traced the muscles along his bicep. I lifted his hand and marveled at its size. My palm drowned in his grip. I examined his long fingers, touching the ridges of his coarse prints, wondering how they'd feel against my cheek. I kneeled next to the couch, still clutching his hand. Oliver had a bit of stubble, "I'm grooming averse," he always jokes. I wondered if the whiskers would tickle my neck. Flushed and dazed, I rested my head on the couch and breathed in. I felt a chill as sweat condensed on my brow and my teeth shuttered. Oliver steered and opened his eyes.

"Are you okay?" he asked

I glanced up to him, smiled feebly and replied "I'm fine."

"You don't look fine."

He slid off the couch, next to me on the floor. Oliver held me firmly as he helped me up and back to the bedroom. He stood over me as I got into bed and laid down. He pulled the covers up to my chin and sat by my side.

"So we're playing tucking tag? I tuck you in, then you tuck me in." I teased.

He smiled down to me, "I'm in your bedroom."

"Yes, you are."

"Not quite what I imagined."

"Really?"

"No pinks or purples. No frills or doilies."

"Pink doilies? Am I supposed to be a sixty-year-old teenager?"

"No mirror either."

"Well, I haven't gotten around to buying one. Besides, I'll have to get an electric drill to install it. Too much trouble to reassure that I'm still ugly."

He smirked and placed his palm on my forehead. "You feel feverish. Where's your thermometer?"

I flushed to his touch and pointed to the dresser, "In the top drawer."

He retrieved the digital device, wiped it with disinfectant and placed in my mouth. Waiting for the thermometer to ding and unable to engage in dialogue, he busied himself with examining the stack of books on my night stand. He picked them up in one grip, placed them on the bed and surveyed each volume. "The Great Gatsby," he nodded. "The Hours." He smiled. "The Perks of Being a Wallflower," he frowned. "Interesting collection," he said. Still no ding, he placed the books in their original position atop my journal, the very journal he purposely avoided. I followed his face with every move, until he rested back into position and returned my gaze. We both willed the thermometer to ding.

"103. You're running a fever," he said.

"What time is it?" I asked.

"4:00 am."

"It's too early for the antibiotics. Maybe some Advil will help." I lifted the covers to get out of bed.

"Where do you think you're going? Back into bed. I'll get you whatever you need."

He gently tucked me in and headed out to the hall. He returned with a green pill in one hand and a glass of water in the other. He watched me take the medicine. On his way out, he paused at the door way to turn off the lights. He looked over his should and said, "I'll be outside if you need anything."

Oliver stayed until the weekend. He took care of me. He'd wake me up to take the antibiotics. He brought me soup and crackers. He checked my temperature and made sure I was hydrated. He read to me to keep me entertained. I enjoyed his company and I didn't want him to leave. Knowing he was in the living room was comforting. His friends picked him up Saturday morning on their way to the beach.

\*\*\*

# August

I can't rid my mind of Oliver. At work, I close my eyes and feel his palm on my forehead. I smell a faint scent of smoke on his breath. Am I reading too much into his affection? Am I setting myself up for disappointment, or am I too cautious because of Mike? Why can't I simply ask Oliver if he likes me? Maybe I can pass him a note in homeroom. Do I like him? Does he factor in with my plans? Should I consider a baby now there's the possibility that Oliver likes me? Maybe I should freeze my eggs? What am I doing?

We work in his office every day. His deadline is approaching and I have tightened the revision schedule. During the day, Oliver prepares a list of changes and I incorporate them in the evening. He diligently sits at his desk and edits copies, scratching out text, correcting tenses, and moving paragraphs. The assertiveness of his conviction is very attractive. The precision with which he manipulates words to convey rationale, the astuteness of his commands, all appeal to me. I watch his lips move as he silently reads. I run my finger over them. The perfect V formation of his cupid's bow captures my attention. It spells victory as my tongue reaches its peak.

***

The last petals on my orchid have fallen off. Two bare stocks sadly stand in the empty flower pot. I put it next to the door as a reminder to take it out with the garbage tomorrow morning. I've been collecting the dry translucent petals. I have them in a pile on my nightstand. I'll take them next weekend into the city and scatter them in Bryant Park.

***

Oliver called me yesterday while I was at work. He usually texts.

"What's wrong?" I asked.

"Why do you think something's wrong?" He replied.

"So nothing's wrong?"

"No. No. Just calling to see if I may come over later?"

"Why?"

"I'm bored."

"People don't come to Long Island because they are bored. People go to Manhattan because they are bored. Aren't you supposed to be working on chapter twenty-five?"

"I need a break."

He arrived at six twenty.

"Nice pajamas." He teased as I greeted him at the door.

"I'm not changing for you. Can I take you coat?"

I placed his damp rain coat on a wire hanger and suspended it from the shower rod to dry.

"I haven't had dinner yet, would you like to join me?" I asked.

"Sure."

We dined on broiled halibut and a warm couscous salad.

"The food is amazing. You should do this professionally."

"It's really not that difficult." I brushed off his compliment. "I enjoy cooking. It's my creative outlet. Taking discrete ingredients and mixing them together to create something totally different than the sum of the parts. It's fascinating how a little bit of salt or a cup of the right kind of wine could transform a dish."

I felt Oliver's gaze. His eyes pierced through me. It didn't mean anything. He was simply being an attentive listener. The blood in my body drained as my face blushed. I hid the crimson tide behind my palm as I cradled my cheek. My hands were sweaty. My head was faint and my breath constrained. I diverted my eyes. I busied myself with the napkin.

"Thank you for a lovely dinner," he said.

"My pleasure. Coffee or tea with dessert?" I asked.

"Tea please."

I walked into the galley kitchen carrying the dirty dished. Oliver brought in the serving plates. I set the kettle on the stove. He arranged cups and saucers on a tray. I quenelled whip creme on slices of chocolate cake. From the corner of my eye, I glanced at Oliver. He looked up and smiled. My body gravitated towards his. I wouldn't describe Oliver as handsome. His hair is always in disarray from ruffling his fingers through it when he's frustrated or hot. His long face leaves his cheeks deflated. Yet, there's an attractive quality about him. The way his face animates with passion when he talks, revealing his age through the crow's feet and horizontal lines along his alabaster brow. His high cheek bones sit prominently below his icy grey eyes that disclose sincerity when he smiles. He seemed genuinely grateful for dinner, genuinely happy to be standing next to me, making tea.

How can I assess Oliver's sincerity? I want him to like me. My desire muddles my judgment. Am I misinterpreting curiosity for care?

The kettles whistled and brought me back to reality. I turned off the stove. Oliver opened sachets and placed individual tea bags in each cup. I filled them with boiling water. Instinct synchronized our movement. Our hands grazed by mistake. An electric wave blasted through my limbs. I hesitated with the kettle in midair. He reached over and took it from my hand.

"Are you alright?" He asked.

I closed my eyes and looked away.

"Oliver, I'm at an impasse in my life. My mind isn't working properly. It's foggy with self-doubt and lots of other shit. That's why I left Chicago. To clear my head. I don't need you fucking with it."

"I don't understand."

"To you, a smile is just a smile. You're probably being polite. But to my fucked-up mind, it's an invitation. When you smile at me, I think you like me. Then, I start to wonder why do you like me. Do you find me cute? witty? eccentric? And that's when I get self-conscious and fixate on every little gesture. I can't deal with this. It would be much simpler if you were an ass?"

"An ass?"

"Yes, a complete asshole. Just stop being so fucking nice."

"First, sorry for being so fucking nice. Second, I can see how a smile could be misconstrued. A kiss, however, shouldn't be confusing."

"A kiss?"

"Yes. If I were to kiss you, there shouldn't be any confusion regarding my intentions."

"Do you want to kiss me?"

"Yes."

"Okay?"

"Does that mean I'm allowed to kiss you?"

"Yes." I smiled invitingly.

My back was to the sink. My hands rested on the edge of the counter. Oliver was facing me. He moved in closer. He placed his right hand on the counter next to my waist. He cupped my face with his left hand. His thumb caressed my chin. At the perfect height difference, he leaned in.

"Stop," I said.

"What?" He hovered an inch from my face.

"What do you want me to do?"

"What do you mean?"

"Should I just passively receive your kiss? Do I reciprocate? Are you expecting encouraging um and ah? What do I do while you kiss me?"

A broad smile emerged on his face. "Why don't you just enjoy it," he said.

"You're very sure of yourself."

"Shut up and let me kiss you."

He pressed his lips to mine. He applied slight pressure to my chin and parted my lips. He inhaled and stole my breath.

\*\*\*

I fell asleep in Oliver's arms last night. I slept to the rhythm of his breathing. My mind was still, void of conflict. My dreams didn't haunt me. I slept through the night. The first time since moving here. I wrapped Oliver around me, assured by his warmth. I slept, and woke up to him still in my bed. I slept, and woke up to him still holding me. I watched him sleep. I felt his heart beat. I inhaled his scent. Oliver filled my bedroom.

"Good morning." He smiled.

I nuzzled my face in his chest. I wanted to be lost in him, to be locked in a time capsule of just that moment. I held onto Oliver, fearing it was a dream. He kissed my neck. Could he hear my frantic heart, for every beat called his name? The rush of blood in my veins solicited his touch. For those brief moments, he was mine.

\*\*\*

I have taken a liking to Morning Side Park since becoming Oliver's research assistant. Nestled on a downward slope, it doesn't seem like much when approached from Amsterdam. I pass by St. Luke's Hospital and The Cathedral of St. John The Devine in search of the plateaued steps leading down to the duck pond. The park is an elongated strip with the majority of the landscape at eye level. I span the entire park in my panoramic view. I select a bench across the small water fall. Unlike Riverside, home of dogs of every persuasion, parents let small Schnauzers off their leash in Morning Side. They are free to chase regal geese, who elegantly escape the playful jaws by prancing into the pond. The green water sits four feet away. I wonder how deep it is.

Morning Side Park is peaceful. Children's cheers echo in the back ground from the baseball field and playing grounds.

Up in the horizon, I see the orange awning of Spoonbread Catering and flying buses passing down Manhattan Avenue. Every time I go to Morning Side Park, I lose all sense of time and overstay my welcome. I hastily walk up the slope and emerge from a jungle of daffodils, weeping willows and maple trees to the asphalt streets of upper Manhattan.

Oliver prefers the elevated paths of Riverside. "It's a cardio warm up." He said as we climbed up Riverside Drive and then down to the tennis courts overlooking the Hudson River. We engage in early tennis matches on Saturday mornings and go to Starbucks afterwards. He reached for my hand as we crossed the street. I halted a step behind. He looked back at me and asked.

"Does this bother you?"

"No, but it feels abnormal."

"Get used to it." He smiled.

His hand is huge. It completely swallowed mine. It felt safe. I reach for him, now. I hug his arm as we stride side by side. I lay my head against his shoulder. I savor the nearness of our embrace and inhale Oliver with every breath.

He held the door for me as I walked in and place my usual order.

"You come to Starbucks to order regular coffee with four ounces of fat free milk?" He asked.

"Yes." I replied.

"But you can get that from anywhere. A doughnut shop or deli."

"I like their coffee."

"Honestly?"

"Yes."

"Why not make it at home?"

"Because I'm not at home."

"Make it at home and bring it with you."

"Why are we arguing about coffee?"

"Because you ordering a tall regular blend from Starbucks is nonsensical."

"Nonsensical? Only an English professor would use the word nonsensical."

"I'm a lecturer."

"I have a Starbucks loyalty card. I get a free purchase with every twelve transactions."

"Ah, It's a commercial incentive and not the grand quality of their coffee then."

\*\*\*

I keep the fan running all night. I close the bedroom door and turn on the A/C. The fan circulates cold air emitting from the small unit underneath the window. Without the fan, the frigid air hits my feet, while the rest of the room remains hot and stuffy.

I turn off the bedroom TV when Oliver spends the night. He demands complete darkness and quiet. He complains about the clucking sound of the fan. He asked me to decrease the speed, but it is only effective when turned up high. He's argument is futile. He immediately falls asleep despite the noise. He sleeps on my side of the bed, on the right, next to my nightstand. I keep a small stool on the other side to house my alarm clock and water bottle.

The bed is too small for the both of us. I chose a full-size bed because the mattress was small enough for me to lift. Our bodies entwine to offset the minimum surface, an excuse to embrace.

But the fan is in fact noisy. It gives off an uneven pitch that accelerates and declines throughout the night at random intervals. This morning it broke down and plopped to a complete halt. I gently climbed out of bed and walked over to the window sill. I kneeled down to unplug it. White powdery dust accumulated on the back grid. I carried the fan to the kitchen and took it apart. I cleaned it with disinfectant wipes and put it back together. I turned it on. The motor struggled to push the black plastic blades clockwise, but they did not move. I turned the speed knob by one degree, then another, but nothing happened. I was reaching up to retrieve my tool kit from the broom closet when Oliver walked in.

"What are you doing?" He asked.

"I'm checking out the fan. The damn thing broke down. I bought it only two months ago."

"Return it and get another one."

"I'll just check to see what's wrong."

"You'll void the warranty. I can think of at least three better activities to do besides disassembling a small appliance."

"Uh? Yeah, yeah. Not now babe. This fan is bugging the hell out me. I want to check it out before work."

"Fine. I need a cigarette anyway."

He walked out of the kitchen. Twenty minutes later, he stood in the living room, freshly showered and dressed. He pulled the strap of his messenger bag over his head as I walked in.

"I thought you were smoking."

"I'll have it on the way to the station. I'm meeting Sofie tonight, so I won't be coming over. I'll call you later."

He walked out of the apartment without saying goodbye.

I carried the morning events with me all day. My mind ponders over our dialogue. It examined every detail of the interaction. The way he left and his body language revealed that he was angry, but at what?

***

Oliver didn't contact me until Friday, leaving me to mull over the fan incident for two days.

*Are you coming over?* He texted.

*When?* I replied.

*Today.* He texted back.

I responded, *Saturday would be best.*

*Fine. But come early. We have a lot to do.*

I arrived Saturday at eight thirty. Oliver answered the door. I was surprised to see him dressed. Waking up early on a Saturday, is very unlike him. The smell of fresh coffee and breakfast filled the apartment. "Good morning love," he said.

He kissed my cheek. "I really want to finish the draft today and send it off to Sofie."

I went to my desk and commenced typing. The draft was complete by two. I printed it out and placed it on Oliver's working space. I got up to leave. We didn't speak all day.

"Where are you going?" He asked.

"The draft's on your desk. I am done."

"We've got reservations at eight."

"Reservations for what?"

"A surprise."

I stayed. It was awkward. Oliver continued reviewing the draft in silence. I sat on the couch and watched TV. The volume was turned down to a whisper. He insisted that the sound didn't bother him. But, I didn't mind the muted entertainment. I wasn't focused on the programming. I idly sat there, preoccupied with the events of the week. Was Oliver behaving differently, or am I focusing too much on his nuances and thus viewing his behavior differently? Is he ignoring me, or simply focused on work? If he's ignoring me, then why would he make reservations? Where we are going? Am I dressed properly? I sat in front of the cooking channel perplexed, debating Oliver.

At six forty, he stood up and took off his glasses. He stretched and walked pass me, interrupting my view of the TV, on his way to the bedroom. He closed the door behind him. He emerged thirty minutes later, showered, shaved and dressed in a black suit and shirt. He smelled of cologne. I've never smelled cologne on him before, just soap and mint. He walked to his desk and retrieved his wallet and phone. He turned to me and smiled.

"Are you ready? I've arranged for a town car to pick us up."

"Am I dressed appropriately?" I asked, pointing to my jeans and oversized sweater.

"You're beautiful." He leaned in and kissed me. His cologne was over powering.

We arrived at Gramercy. We walked down five steps to the entrance of a restaurant. The maitre d' took our jackets and seated us in a booth.

"I've asked the chief to prepare something special for the evening. I hope you don't mind." Oliver said. His arm extended along the back of the curved banquette, in a pseudo embrace. "The owner and I have a mutual friend. He was very accommodating."

"What's the occasion?"

"We've been spending every evening in. I thought it would be a nice change. Would you like a drink?"

"No."

"You never break the rules? You can make an exception for tonight."

"Alcohol makes me act weird. I get all talkative and ramble on and on about absolutely nothing. It makes me light headed. I don't like it."

"Fine."

He ordered a whiskey sour.

"So, how's the fan?" He asked.

"I couldn't fix it."

"And now your warranty is void."

"Yes."

He looked at me with a smug expression that said, "You should have listened to me."

"They have an amazing pianist here. He starts at ten. He plays an assortment of classical music and jazz improvisations. I was seven when my parents first took me to the symphony. The piano solo was like a fireworks display in my ears. I used to think that our Steinbach was a huge piece of furniture. After the concert I understood that there was more to the piano then rectangular keys and parallel cords."

"Do you know how to play?" I asked.

Oliver silently sipped his drink.

"That's very impressive," I said.

"I'd believe you, if you didn't have a smirk on your face."

"No. No. I'm serious."

"I take it that you don't play the piano."

"God no. I wish, but I lack the grace and eye hand coordination required to learn an instrument. And I have two left ears."

He frowned inquisitively.

"I can't carry a tune," I explained.

"Ah, I see. So, you never learned how to play music."

"Never."

"Your mother never made you endure excruciating lessons?"

"Nope. My mom never forced me to do anything."

"What did you do after school?"

"Watched a lot of television. Did my homework. Read books. My mom used to give me math exercise books. I spent Saturday afternoons solving math equations."

Oliver had two glasses of Cabernet Sauvignon with his Beef Wellington and a bottle of Prosecco for dessert. He was drunk before we started the cheese course. I asked for the check and called the driver. I helped Oliver out of the booth. He swiftly talked and repeated his word. He walked with a hunch, as oppose to his usual straight posture. We stood up to leave, when he loudly proclaimed, "I have to go to the loo," disturbing the tranquility of the piano player. When he was done, he slid back into the booth. I had to pull him up.

"Come on Oliver. We should leave."

"No, let's stay. Let's dance. You like to dance, remember. You said it gave you an excuse to hold on to me and sway. Come on."

I didn't tell him that. I wrote it in my journal.

The car drove us back to Oliver's. I helped him out of his suit jacket and put him to bed.

When I got home, I went straight to the bedroom. My journal was in the top drawer of the dresser. I opened it to that entry and tore out the page. I took it to the kitchen and placed it on the open flame of the stove. I watched it burn to ash. The ink writings darkened with the rise of the temperature. The words vanished into the soot background. The fan still sat on the counter, plugged in and set to level three. I took a butter knife and inserted it between the narrow openings of the face grid. I pushed the blade to the left. The motor growled. I pushed the blade further. I felt the thrust of the machine. I pulled out the knife and the fan whizzed into motion.

\*\*\*

Next day at one, I got a text message. "I'm sorry," flashed on my phone. Oliver was down stairs with a bouquet of lilies. I let him in.

"I was an ass last night. I'm sorry."

"You were drunk."

"Yes. I don't remember much, but I woke up with a hangover and still in my clothes. I knew I had to apologize."

"So, you're apologizing for the sake of an apology, not because you regret acting like a jerk."

"Zoe, love, I wanted us to have a good time and regret that my behavior ruined the evening. And for that, I am truly, sincerely sorry."

I smiled. I didn't know what else to do. He did apologize, but I wanted to continue the discussion. I accepted his apology but he didn't care to learn why I was angry. I knew he read my journal. How could he just pick it up and read it? Why was he rummaging through my dresser in the first place? What else did he read? But I didn't pursue the matter further. This line of questioning would have irritated Mike. I missed Oliver. I missed waking up to him. I missed cooking for him. Even if we were apart for only three days. I was excited when he asked me to come over. I looked forward to being with him. And there he was, standing in my doorway, apologizing. So, I said nothing. I silenced my doubts with a smile. He came in and stayed for dinner.

"This is so good. Would it be impolite if I were to lick my fingers?" He said.

"I'll consider it a complement."

"My God. What is this?"

"Teriyaki. I added a bit of orange zest and orange juice to complement to duck. Besides that, it is simple, straight forward Teriyaki."

Oliver ran his index finger through the sauce on his plate. He ravenously licked his finger tip and lips. I was pleased he enjoyed my cooking.

"What are going to do with your fingers?" He asked as he grabbed my hand and placed my fingers in his mouth, sucking them one at a time. He stood up and firmly held my face. He leaned down and sucked all the teriyaki off my lips.

"Even better," he said.

"You're crazy. Do you know that? Absolutely, utterly crazy." I managed to say between girlish giggles.

I was no longer angry.

\*\*\*

# September

Oliver and I were in bed. We laid on our sides. We silently stared at each other over an invisible ravine. Both us too timid to leap across. I reached out and rested my hand on his chest. The collar of his polo shirt draped my fingers, revealing a triangular patch of skin. I pressed my lips to his bare flesh and smiled.

I am a noisy person by nature. My knees creak when I walk upstairs. My jaw pops when I talk. I have a hurried stride. I pound my feet as I walk. I favor comfortable shoes with rubber soles. They squeak against hard floors. I'm loud and my voice peaks with enthusiasm. Yet, when I'm with Oliver, I am calm. My pace quiets. My body slows down to savor every moment we share. We don't need to speak. We decipher each other's thoughts by virtue of a smile. I browsed his Facebook photographs one afternoon. When he's with friends, a smile fills his face. His lips curve up exposing his teeth. Joy livens his eyes. His light grey pupils melt into the whites and peek from behind narrow slits. The force of his smile creases his eyelid. But with colleagues, his smile is contrite. He focuses on the camera, ignoring the company.

We don't use words to express our feelings. I hear 'I care for you' when he holds my hand, when he looks at me across a crowded room and know that I'm bored with a party and want to leave. 'I pine for you' is exhibited rather than said. The rush of his kiss. The intensity of his embrace. On the couch, watching TV, he rests his head on my shoulder. He breathes against my neck, announcing 'I am yours'. We don't need pedestrian phrases like 'I love you'. People use it in the context of 'I love sushi'. It's void of meaning. They don't even bother with the word love, instead they say 'I heart sushi', or make a gesture with their fingers. How can I say 'I love you' when my feelings for him is much more than my affinity for sushi. How can I possibly say that I'm jealous of the air he breaths. I want to consume him, completely. I want all of him to be mine. No, I tell him nothing. When we are together, I remain silent.

\*\*\*

It's sad how Rockville Centre is disintegrating as the economy crumbles. Independent stores are closing down, regardless of goods or service. Two delicatessens have gone out of business. Restaurants and bars strive on departed retailers. New establishments open. Existing ones expand into vacant adjacent locations. The refurbish furniture boutique that sold me the nightstand is going out of business. They have a large 'Everything Must Go' sign in their window. Oliver and I dropped by. He bought a China tea pot and hand carved wooden frame. I considered buying a vintage 1962 red and white Schwinn Jaguar bike.

"Are you going to ride it?" Oliver asked.

"I don't think so. It's beautiful. I'll mount it on the wall."

The weather condoles the demise of main street USA. Clouds overshadow the roads, but it doesn't rain. The sun refuses to come out and witness the death of independent shops selling hardware, luggage, optical glasses, and children's clothes. Leaves bow down to honor the fallen and mourn the loss of summer. One lone rose stands proudly, persevering against the drop of temperatures, holding on to the hope of sunshine.

\*\*\*

Oliver has completed his manuscript. He's sent the final copy to his editor.

"What are you going to do now?" I asked.

"Get it published and enjoy the accomplishment," he replied.

"Are you going back to the UK?"
"For the Holiday's, possibly."
He didn't ask me to go with him.
"Columbia asked me to stay on for next semester."
So, he's staying in New York.

To celebrate, Oliver hosted a dinner party for his friends and colleagues. I haven't met any of them. I wonder if he has told them about us. I offered to put together a menu but Oliver insisted on having the event catered. "I want you to enjoy yourself," he said. I felt very guilty, leaving all the planning to him, but he wouldn't let me help.

I debated the dress code all week. I went shopping. I bought a slim black suit dress, an emerald green sleeveless pleated cocktail dress, and navy wide trousers with matching silk blouse. I hung a full-length mirror on the closet door. I paired each ensemble with different shoes and accessories. I photographed myself in the different options and examined them attentively to select the best one. I was nervous about meeting his friends. I wanted to impress them. I finally opted for black tapered trousers and aubergine sweater, with an old pair of ballet flats and a cross body purse. I wrapped myself with a large floral pashmina. I was ready by one o'clock. The dinner wasn't until eight. I didn't know what to do for the remaining seven hours. I underdressed and took a nap. My enthusiasm wavered over the day. I had sushi for lunch. I took an extend lavish shower. I moisturized my face and body. I deliberately forgot about the party until it was time to leave. I couldn't escape it on the train ride. I doubted my choice of clothes. I obsessed over discussion topics, fearing I wouldn't have anything intelligent to say. What if someone asks me about the last book I have read? What will they think when I tell them it's about the cognitive process of creativity? What if they ask me about my job? Should I tell them that I'm a project coordinator? Would it be pretentious to say that I'm a business consultant? Why did I care so much about their judgement? Moving to New York and working in a mediocre job was my choice. I shouldn't be concerned with the opinion of strangers. For all I know these people might be casual acquaintances with Oliver. But why would he invite them to a celebratory dinner if they weren't important to him. Why am I assuming that their opinion would have any bearing on Oliver? He knows me. He knows who I am and how I am. Preoccupied with the mental arguments in my head, I sprayed Coco Mademeoiselle on my wrists. It smelled safe. It smelled familiar.

I arrived at seven forty. I was early, although I stopped at Columbus circle for a box of Godiva chocolates. A young woman in a black pencil skirt and white dress shit answered the door.

"May I take your wrap?" She asked.

"Where's Oliver?"

"He's getting ready. Can I get you a drink?"

"Sparkling water, with a twist of lime please."

I entered the living room. Most of the furniture had been removed. Couches and chairs were pushed against the wall. A bar was setup in the corner next to the kitchen, A man in a similar uniform was wiping glasses. I was still holding the box of chocolates, not sure what to do with it. I took my drink and went to the window where our desks used to be. I stared out to Seventieth Street. I was the first guest to arrive. Oliver appeared a few minutes later. I was relieved to see him in slacks and a cardigan. He kissed me on the cheek. I gave him the chocolates. "You didn't have to do that," he said.

His friends arrived in pairs. Everyone there knew everyone there, or at least someone there, Oliver. I, too, knew Oliver. But not the Oliver there at the party. He looked the same, sounded the same, and behaved the same. Yet, he didn't seem the same. Something was different. I had never seen him interacting with other people. It's always been only the two of us. Yet, there I was, expected to share him with a room full of his acquaintances. I only knew him in the context of us. It was difficult to perceive him as a friend, a son, a brother, a human being. To see him as he is when he's not with me.

Oliver introduced me to the first group to arrive, Ryan, Campbell, Matt and his girlfriend, Camille.

"This is Zoe. She helped me finish the manuscript on time."

"You're studying English lit too?" Asked Camille.

"No," I replied.

They were graduate students. They talk amongst themselves. I stood by, not totally oblivious to their discussion on the feminine subtext in Shakespeare. I took small sips of my drink and nodded attentively. I soon walked away. I jumped from one group to the next. Parents exchanging preschool experiences. Academics discussing the difficulty of tenure. Twenty somethings debating the merits of craft beer. All was engaged in banal dinner party banter. I stood in the corner, observing Oliver and waiting for the evening to end.

\*\*\*

# October

The worst thing in life is to covet something you'll never have. You spend every day mourning its loss, although it was never yours. Your heart aches with desire. Why do we lust after such things? Why do we convince ourselves that we deserve them? Why do we tether out happiness to false hope? Hope is a remorseless culprit. That dim light of maybe, keeps you pining for the impossible until all you want is to crush that hope, defeat the parasite that feeds on your needs till you need no more.

I want to be loved, but I must love in return. Will Oliver teach me how to love? Why do I covet love, when I've never known what it is? Is it a physiological need like hunger? Why do I yearn for the warmth of an embrace, the comfort of a knowing smile, the soothing sound of a lover calling my name? When hungry, your body gurgles to signal that it requires nourishment. Yet, you can't possibly know that you are hungry for cake unless you have tasted it before. Maybe it is envy. Like a hungry vagabond, I press my face against the window of other couples' happiness, salivating over confections I know nothing of. Maybe it is greed, because society has denied me love? I've never been taught how to be loved and reciprocate it. My parents never said I Love You to one another, at least not in my presence. Never a kiss, not even goodbye on the cheek. Never a hug, not even to hold hands. Were they happy? Are they happy? Why did they marry if there weren't in love? Why would they remain together if they are not in love? Is it familiarity, a fear of change?

I'm tired. I'm continuously tired. I'm tired of making all the decisions. I'm tired of baring all the responsibilities. I want to be weak. I want to break down. I want to be vulnerable, knowing that someone will pick up the pieces when I shatter. I can no longer contain my thoughts or stop them from roaming freely in my mind. I find no refuge in books. The text has become words with no meaning. I have lost myself beyond the escape of fictional lives. There's no solace, but I continue to read. Perhaps it was a poor choice, resuming Comrac McCathy's *Child of God*. I cry for Lester. I pain for him. I, too, desire to look into my window to see a warm home and a happy family. I, too, fill the void with illusions. What does it say about me when I sympathize with a necrophiliac killer? Yet, I understand his plight, as I've always done with my fictional friends. When I was younger, I would read all night, unwilling to put down a book until I completed it. I consumed many summer days in movie marathons. I closed my eyes and injected myself in the make believe, begrudgingly ejecting the fantasy when my mother interrupted.

"Why don't you go outside and do something? Go to the mall," she said.

"What am I supposed to do at the mall?" I asked.

"Hang out with friends. Do whatever kids your age do."

I have learned to curb my appetite, balancing fact with fiction and dispersing my literary excursions. Living with the promise of fiction to ease the pain of living a life I do not desire.

We all escape at one point in our lives. Teenagers seek refuge in rebellion. We live in constant fear of becoming our parents. But we can't escape our genetic making. Students daydream and skip school to go to the movies. Employees persevere on fumes of retirement. We live our lives running away from one reality towards the next. We envision a future, something different, something new. Even those of us who are content, escape in their dreams. They retreat to foreign lands and alternative realities. Life is the pursuit of the imaginary, seeking adventure in the unknown.

\*\*\*

It's quite difficult to wake up every day, climb out of bed, and go to a job for which you have no passion. You mindlessly executive tasks, but you can't force yourself to care. You do an excellent job. Yet void of enthusiasm, you can't be concerned. No passion. No concern. No care. We never want more of what we don't desire. Achieving more, in this case, has a negative effect. It's clutter. It's unnecessary. It's unwanted. If I'm competent at my job, why does it matter whether I want more out of it or not? Lack of desire for more responsibilities and promotions does not diminish my ability to do my job well. I am the perfect employee, never challenging the status quo, happy with my placement in the hierarchy. My indifference should be hailed and encouraged.

I'll send Brian an e-mail this weekend to let him know that I'm coming back to Chicago. I'll return to the firm.

\*\*\*

My body hungers for human contact. I thirst for you. I want to withdraw to the sanctity of your presence. I miss you.

I like touching Oliver, for an embrace is more intimate than sex. I sneak my hand under his shirt to hold him. I press my face to his neck. In his arms, I am home. I am happy.

\*\*\*

I can't sleep. I have turned off the TV because the dimmed tones of the shopping channel don't put me to sleep anymore. I close my bedroom door. I turn off the lights. I lay in bed, in total darkness, but sleep does not come. I stare at the ceiling. My eyes adjust to the faint moonlight projected through the blinds. I see the vertical crack in the ceiling plaster. I wear a light blue satin eye mask with colorful peace signs, to force my eyes shut. But I still don't fall asleep. Dark circles have formed under my eyes. They're more half circles than full ones, maybe even crescent shaped. Why are they called dark circles? I'm tired, yet I cannot sleep.

I close my eyes and see Long Beach. I feel the warm velvety sand under my bare feet. I walk to the edge of the water. Effervescent waves brushed the shore, licking my toes as they sink further below the tide. The swishing waves against my body are a harmonized symphony of serenity, massaging away my anxiety. How wonderful it feels to be swept away, fully and thoroughly submerges, engulfed by the tide. The ocean consumes me. I am safe. I'm guarded. I fall asleep.

***

New York is expecting a super storm. Temperatures are too warm for snow. Yet, authorities expect rain to accumulate into floods and eight miles per hour wind to cause massive destruction. Constant chatter about the storm and the necessary precautions fills morning TV shows. I was called into work this Saturday afternoon to help with disaster recovery preparations.

We had an emergency conference call to review our D/R procedures and ensure that everyone was aware of their responsibilities. Support engineers started an offline backup of critical data late Friday. It was later relayed to an offsite location in Denver. We reviewed lesson learned from a previous incident two years earlier. Charles wanted to make sure we don't face the same issues as before. We reviewed our emergency tag-contact list. It contained the names, addresses, and contact information of everyone working in IT. Each person on the list was required to call the next in line and pass on set messages if predefined emergency events occur. Some phone numbers were updated. Administration rented additional generators and had them installed at the residences of our CEO and financial controller. Management agreed with two centrally located hotels to tentatively book meeting facilities to act as a disaster recovery war room, in case of power outages. Charles tagged two colleagues who lived near the office with the responsibility of manually powering down the data center, if flood water should reach the premises.

Charles drove me home after we were done. It was 10:30 at night.

"Thank you for coming in Zoe. Your organizational skills helped us a lot," Charles said.

"It's my job," I replied.

"Are you aware of the evacuation zones and shelters in your area?"

"Yes. I received a flyer early June at the beginning of hurricane season."

"Good. So, you're all set?"

"I think so. I've been to the market a couple of times. I've stocked up on water and canned foods. I've gotten batteries, a flash light and lantern, as well as candles. I have a hand crank radio and first aid kit. Once a planner, always a planner." I smiled.

"Good girl."

Driving west on Merrick, we passed bars bustling with Halloween parties. Meteorologists recommended securing glass panels with masking tape at least six inches wide. One other apartment besides my own had the cream X marks on their windows.

"You know, they said everyone south of Merrick should evacuate," Charles said.

"I checked with the neighbors. They said we should be fine. I live on the third floor, I don't reckon the water will get that high."

"You're welcome to come and stay with Angela and me. You can bunk in with the girls. They'd be happy to have you."

"Thank you Charles. That's very kind of you. But I'll be fine."

I went to CVS the next day and bought additional batteries. I got cheese crackers, cookies, potato chips, and condensed milk for coffee. I put an additional T formation of tape on the windows facing south. I laid out all the supplies on the dining table, for easy access in the dark. I cleared the bottom of the hallway closet for shelter, if required and I charged my phone.

Super Storm Sandy hit New York at 8:00 pm on Monday, 29th October.

It was an accumulation of heavy rain at first, steadily and slowly. The wind picked up speed eighty minutes into the storm and the lights started to flicker. I unplugged all appliances and turned off the lights. I headed to the bedroom with a best seller novel for a bit of levity. I left my bedside lamp on and settled into reading. A few minutes later, the lights went out.

I sat in the darkness, to conserve batteries. I didn't know how long the blackout was going to last. I got up and crept to the window. I peeked out from behind the blinds. It was black as tar outside. No lights. No shining stars. No beaming moon. The sound was frightening. The blinding darkness amplified the impact of howling wind. I couldn't see the destruction that was occurring, but the sound of gusting air bombing rain against the walls gave it away. Not knowing what I will face when the lights returned, frightened me most of all.

I turned on the radio to the news. There were no songs playing on the other channels as I surfed by. I clutched the black plastic box. It emitted whispers in my ear as I slept.

\*\*\*

I woke up the next day and the lights were on. I turned off the radio and checked my phone. There was no cell service. I walked around the apartment, plugging in electric devices. I checked the refrigerator. It was working and nothing inside had spoiled. I plugged the router and waited for the system to boot. Thankfully I had television and internet services. I turned on the TV.

Sandy stormed though the Tristate area, ripping out boardwalks, tearing down trees and power lines, washing away homes, and covering roads with sand and debris. The images were the same on all channels, destruction and despair. I looked outside the living room window. It continued to rain. No one was outside in the streets. I couldn't hear any voices from the neighbors.

I spent the entirety of Tuesday tethered to the TV set. Flood waters reached the office. The building was closed until the city cleared it safe. The loading dock, elevator shaft and other parts of the structure below street level incurred water damage. Beachside cities were devastated. Long Beach was evacuated. Residents didn't return until after the holidays. The boardwalk crumbled under the force of heavy winds. Fourteen feet tidal waves over took Lower Manhattan and Brooklyn, flooding subway stations and streets. Flood water and fire damage wrecked blocks of homes in the Rockaways. Despite the destruction, the loss, the sorrow, there was a sense of perseverance. This too shall pass.

I surveyed Rockville Centre. It stopped raining on Wednesday, but the city was still wet. Puddles accumulated at every corner. Bare tree branches stretched out like arthritic fingers. The wind blew away all the leaves. Bright green algae covered tree trunks. The clouds casted a shadow upon the streets. None of the traffic lights worked. Crossing intersections was a challenge. I trod up Park Avenue in my rubber boots and heavy coat. Crowds congested the city. Delis, restaurants and bars were all packed with patrons. Cars lined the streets. A lone trick-or-treater walked next to his mother in a spiderman costume. The only reminder that it was Halloween. I walked to Starbucks. A long line extended to the back entrance. Teenagers and children of all ages littered tables, congregating around power outlets to charge their mobile devices and use the free Wi-Fi. I eavesdropped on the surrounding conversations. A couple from Freeport had a flooded basement. A mother from Belmont was talking to her husband on the phone. They didn't have any power. She was on her way to Lynbrook to check on her mother and borrow extra blankets. A man from Merrick was on a petrol run, filling his tank and an extra canister of gas for his generator. Anne, the barista, lived in Rockville Center. Her area lost power when the wind uprooted a tree. It fell into her neighbor's front yard, talking down the power lines.

I got my coffee and went back home.

# November

Damage caused by Sandy was far more reaching, displacing hundreds of families. They took shelter in hotels. It battered state roadways causing delays in the delivery of groceries and gas to distribution centers. Coupled with an increase in demand to fuel generators, long lines ensued at the pumps. I had ample supply to last a couple of weeks, yet news reports of food shortage cause me to panic. I went to the market. Shelves were bare, void of bread, soup, milk and eggs. I bought oranges, apples, and extra candles.

Several people from work were impacted. Nancy had to stayed with her son in White Plains for three weeks because fallen branches and trees closed roads leading to her neighborhood and cut off power. Colleagues commuting from New Jersey, Connecticut and upstate New York worked from home because of gas shortages. The office was closed for two weeks. Our Disaster Recovery preparations were successful. It took us only twenty-four hours to setup a cold backup site in Denver. Charles, however, wanted a more rigorous plan for future incidents. I had a new project to keep me busy through the holidays.

***

I climbed out of the underground platform at Penn station and walked the length from Seventh Avenue to Eighth. A discreet staircase appeared to my right. It broke through the array of train station offerings, Au Bon Pain next to an Auntie Anne's Pretzels. I climbed the ten steps and proceeded along a narrow corridor. I stopped momentarily at Hudson Books to see whether the new issue of the Harvard Business Review was in stock. It was not. I continued on my quest. The corridor opened to Amtrack's main concourse. Bodies cluttered the large terminal. Back packers, worn with fatigue, sat on the ground and rested against the grimy walls, waiting for the next leg of their journey. Suitcases of every size and disposition rolled across the tiled floors. Lines of humans stood dejected and haphazard under the huge notice board, scanning the flicking data for information about arriving and departing trains. The station was firmly tucked underneath Madison Square Garden, there was no sign of the weather outside. The florescent lighting concealed the time of day. I moved along the hall, passing souvenir vendors, TGI Friday's and newsstands. I saw my destination. Housed in its own conclave next to Thirty-third and Eighth Avenue exit was the sole Krispy Kreme doughnut outlet in New York City. No 'Hot' sign was visible, yet the golden puffy Os greeted on comers from behind glass stands. I placed my order. Every time I venture into Manhattan, I stop at Krispy Kreme for a glazed doughnut, the taste of home.

Every Sunday morning, my father and I drove to the nearest Krispy Kreme. He'd get a regular coffee and I, a glazed doughnut. We'd sit at an empty table next to a window and people watch. We seldom spoke. He'd ask an occasional 'How's school?' and 'Anything new?' between sips of coffee. Before leaving, my father would buy a dozen of powdered cake doughnuts. We each had one for breakfast the following week. We hopscotched between cafes as outlets closed down over the years, until we could no longer find any Krispy Kreme shops in Charlotte. My father continued to buy our dozen doughnuts from grocery stores. They'd stack the powdery white goodies in paper bags.

When I left home for college, I continued the daily doughnut and coffee ritual each morning. It was difficult to keep the tradition after graduating and moving to Chicago. I staggered away from fried sweets and adhered to fresh fruit and yogurt for breakfast. Yet, whenever I was home, dad and I sat at the kitchen table, ate doughnuts, drank coffee, and talked about nothing. We simply enjoyed each other's company.

***

You wake up every day wishing for something you cannot have. You dwell on that one thing. You fixate on it. Your heart aches with loss. You can't breathe. You struggle to live. You shed tears then you push them away, deep down into your consciousness. You make no plans. You discard the future. You live one day at a time and avoid that one thing you don't have and can't live without.

You spend time searching for something, anything, but you never find it. You drown in a sea of discovery. You reject alternatives and hold out for that one thing. You thrash and kick. You grasp for any rescue. You reach out for the nearest object, convinced that it's your salvation, knowing that it is a mirage.

It's that feeling again, emptiness. People wonder why we over eat and drink. It is to fill the void and numb the pain. At first, we want to feel anything, even pain, to replace the nothingness. Soon the pain becomes too intense to handle. It reminds us that we are still alive. We crave the numbness to forget the pain, to forget the loneliness, as if it has abated. The more we drink, the sooner we forget, or so we hope. Hope fools us all.

***

It was raining tonight as I walked home. I had my backpack on, freeing my hands. It wasn't heavy rain, so I discarded my umbrella. The city had restored traffic lights after the damage caused by Sandy. Those along Sunrise are LED. The ones along Merrick are not. On sunny afternoons, it is difficult to distinguish which color is on. I was waiting for the light to change at the intersection of Park Avenue and Merrick Road. The hanging lights danced in the breeze of this November evening. In my peripheral view, I saw the n4 bus approaching from the east. A small crowd collected at the bus stop on the corner where I stood. I looked up, the light was green. I stepped off the sidewalk and proceeded to cross Merrick. The bus's loud siren jolted me back into reality. I jumped backwards onto the curb, confused at the commotion. I examined the traffic lights. The one above Park was red. The one above Merrick was green. I identified the different colors, but I couldn't process their meaning. I wasn't sure if I should cross the street or wait. I glanced at the pedestrian light. It was red. I stood there waiting for it to turn.

\*\*\*

It's interesting how sadness and despair physically manifest themselves. My heart is atrophied with sorrow. I thought it would be easier to forget you, if I hated you. I scrutinized your every flaw. The flaws I love. I close my eyes to see you. I see your weathered tan leather briefcase. The one your old girlfriend gave you. You kept it although you are no longer with her. I see the ligature marks of the bungee rope you use to lash the bag to your bike. I see your hand and long fingers. I see your vintage Breitling watch. The same one your grandfather wore. You wear it on your right wrist because you are left-handed. I see the empty Dr. Pepper can you use as an ashtray. When I breathe in, I smell the cigarette smoke. I see the ceramic mug that holds your pens and pencils. "The correct pen is a crucial writing tool. For taking notes, you need something that writes smoothly and swiftly glides across paper, leaving no smudges. For editing and revisions, you need a stark colored pencil. For handwritten correspondence, you should use a felt tip or gel ink, better yet a fountain pen. Selecting the appropriate writing instrument is akin to choosing proper fonts in your word processor. Words convey meaning. The color of the ink, type of paper and calligraphy convey method and functionality." You often talked about your writing instruments.

I see your hand reach up and adjust your reading glasses.

Both lens are visibly scratched. You leave them on your face when you nap. You carry them in your pocket without a case. You reluctantly put them on when you fail to read fine print. You said, "They make me feel old." I see the stacks of books on your desk. I flip through the earmarked pages. I see all the things I loved to hate about you.

"Take off your shirt." I told you.

"Why?" You asked.

"There's something I want to do."

I smiled and pushed you down on the bed. Light brown blemishes covered your torso. Coffee stains on white paper. I traced them with my finger, connecting the dots.

"These are actually flaws, yet they denote beauty." I said. I bent down and kissed the one nearest your naval. "So, If I were to kiss each and every one of them." I worked my way you your chest until I reached the last one next to your Adam's apple, "I'd be loving your flaws as well as your beauty."

I force myself to hate you, to detest the idea of you. I wreck with loss not hatred. I'm remorseful. I covet the warmth of love. I fill my heart with images of you. Your smile gives me reason to rejoice. The sound of your voice brings me comfort. But this is no more. The site of you steals my heart of reasons to beat. I miss the shelter of your embrace. I urn for the safety of you to make me whole again. But I don't have you. I never did. I never will.

\*\*\*

# December

I saw the old lady in a funny hat today. I don't want to be the old lady. Do I not desire to grow old? Or is it the loneliness? What's the alternative, growing old with someone? Is this why I desire love? To have a companion along the rest of my life? To have someone mourn my death? Yet, the notion of being with the same person forever is daunting. Can I sustain such an affair? The only long-term relationship I've had is with my parents. Was this by choice? They are my parents. They gave me life. They raised me to their best ability. Their actions are born of concern. My father's unobtrusive demeanor gave me allowance to be independent and opinionated. I became the woman I wanted to be. My mother's overbearing curiosity and judgmental nature was never evil. She wanted me to avoid the mistakes she made. She wanted me to make the right decisions. She wanted me to have the life she always wanted for me. My father wanted me to learn from my mistakes. He wanted me to have the life I wanted for myself, mishaps and all. I've always known this. I love them despite them, and they love me despite me. Our love is compulsory. It is instinctive.

None of my other relationships lasted for decades, not even my friendship with Alison. Why would I continue to love a single man for the rest of my life? Why did I think Mike could have been that man? Did I love Mike? I was attracted to him, but I didn't know who he was. I never enjoyed spending time with him. When we were together, we each did our own thing, separately. We simply occupied the same space. Maybe that's how relationships endure. Couples learning to coexist despite their differences. Maybe I could have done that with Mike. I was willing to try to coexist with him. Yet, I'm neglecting to acknowledge that Mike didn't want a relationship. He wanted to move on, to move back. He never considered an alternative with us together. I was simply a pitstop. No, Mike and I wouldn't have endured.

Why do couples coherently coexist? People evolve at different rates. Do we grow at the same pace and in the same direction because we are together? It's only rational that we'd grow apart. What kind of life would that be? Growing old with a stranger. Maybe being the old lady isn't the worst option. A couple that moves away from one another with each day they share. Why would you mourn my passing? Why would you mourn the death of a person you do not know? You'd cry for the loss of a soul. A commuter shedding a tear at the lifeless body of a dog lying in the road. The image evokes saddens in your hearts. But, it's simply the death of another stray dog.

Why do my parents stay together? Why do all the couples choose to remain in a relationship? The notion of being alone scares people into becoming couples. Better miserable together than alone. Which is worse? You're never truly alone unless you spend eternity by yourself. And you're never in a relationship unless you spend eternity as a couple. One person cannot experience both to decide which is worse.

\*\*\*

Hope's a dagger through the heart. Hemorrhage starts once you withdraw hope from the wound. Shards remain embedded in the flesh, sprouting new hope that stabs still. Despair rusts the soul and erodes it away. Hope and happiness bled out of my heart years ago. I was left with nothing. You came along and filled the void, but now you are gone. When the image of you fades, I fiddle with our memories. I reminisce until I hear your voice, I feel your breath.

I see you in my journal. I see you in my dreams, in my fantasies. I love you with every cell of my being. I long for you. I crave your lips, your fingertips. I miss the smell of you, the hint of tobacco from your lone daily cigarette, masked with menthol lozenge. I ache for your warmth, for the safety of knowing you are at arm's length. I miss the rhythm of your heart. Each breath drawn from my lungs beckons your name. I kiss your neck, your arms, your chest, your feet. I love you completely and partially. To be with you is life. To be without you is death. To never have you is despair.

My desire for you is physically painful, like I'm severing my own limb. It's an itch I cannot reach. It worsens until I cannot breathe. My heart is as heavy as a cinder block. My legs and arms are stiff with grief. I will them to move. A step takes the effort of a marathon. I move one foot in front of the other, but I get nowhere. My heart beats despite me. We are pushed into this world, forced to live a life we haven't created. We accumulate memories, then our lives become an effort to retain those moments. With a lack of life, we urn, we want, we desire, we fantasize. A constant remembrance of what we don't have.

Life is wasted on me. I am nothing more than useless consumption of air and space. I wish I could give my minutes to the dying to bid farewell to their loved ones. I wish I could give my days to the young to remain innocent a bit longer. I wish I could give my years to the wise to use in devising good for humanity. But my minutes, days and years are not mine to give away. They are my burden to bare.

The darkness has taken over. It fills my consciousness. My mind surrenders to the image. I focus on the pendulum. The swinging motion regulates my breathing. Right, inhale. Left, exhale. I continue with the journals to calm my nerves. When I don't write, notions pull me in all directions, thoughts of loneliness, sorrow, gloom. A continuum of despair fills my being. I surrender to the darkness. I welcome the image. It is my salvation. It is my end.

*What does this mean?* wondered Patricia. She turned over the last journal, looking for missing pages and additional clues. There was nothing more than the last word '*end.*' It was twenty past four in the morning. She stayed up all night reading the diaries. Her guilt about violating Zoe's privacy dissipated with each page. She moved from the bed to an armchair next to the window. The Zoe she found on the pages of those journals astounded Patricia. Every word she read was a surprise. Zoe never mentioned Mike or Oliver, or the circumstances leading to her New York move. Zoe never spoke of the *darkness* to Patricia.

She got out of the chair and stood in front of the window. She looked out to the hotel's parking lot. It was pitch dark. No remnants of the moon or stars were visible. Her only companion was the fleeting lights of a passing LIRR train. Patricia couldn't steady her mind. She was certain that something terrible had happened to Zoe. Her imagination projected morbid theories. The journals left her with many unanswered questions. She resigned to sleep off her anxiety and seek answers in the morning.

She didn't get much sleep. Zoe preoccupied her dreams. Every time Patricia closed her eyes, she'd see a seven-year-old Zoe playing in the backyard, dressed in purple shorts and a Benji t-shirt. She hopped over a plastic clown head that sprayed water out of the top. She smiled and shouted, "Look at me mommy. See how high I can jump." Patricia wasn't certain whether this was a memory or a dream.

She got up at nine. Her body ached from the restless night. She took a warm shower to ease her muscles. She stopped at the adjacent CVS for aspirin. She walked to Starbucks for coffee.

Sitting at a table across of the register, Patricia couldn't stop thinking about Zoe. 'I'm making a big deal out of nothing. So, she got her heart broken. It's probably not the first time, nor will it be the last. Maybe Oliver took her to Europe. Why didn't she mention Mike or Oliver? Why did she break up with them? Where are all of her possessions? Are they in storage? If so, does this mean she's coming back to New York? Then why did she leave the apartment?' The journals didn't offer any explanation. She wiped her brow and sighed audibly with frustration.

"Having a bad day?" Asked a barista cleaning the table next to her.

"Yes. I didn't get much sleep last night," replied Patricia.

"Coffee will help. Hi, I'm Anne by the way." She extended her arm to shake Patricia's hand.

"Patricia!"

"I haven't seen you before."

"I'm visiting from Charlotte. Actually, I believe you can help me. I'm looking for information about my daughter. Maybe you know her." Patricia reached for her phone and showed Anne a picture of Zoe.

"Oh, you're Zoe's mom. How's she doing?"

"I don't know. She's missing."

"I'm sorry to hear that. She used to come in everyday and ordered the same thing, Tall Pike in a Grande cup. I haven't seen her since the holidays."

Patricia smiled in a show of gratitude and shifted her attention back to Zoe. Her intuition screamed, 'something horrible has happened,' although she had no evidence to corroborate this notion. Her eyes teared up. She put on her sunglasses for some privacy. She cried at the baffling journal entries. The handwriting was Zoe's, but the words and sentiment did not match the image she had of her daughter.

She called Jose and asked if he still had Zoe's books. She passed by and collected them in the shopping trolley. She took them back to the hotel. She searched the books for traces of Zoe. The eclectic assortment of novels, essays, short stories, and poetry chapbooks gave nothing away. They simply conveyed Zoe's zeal for reading and her respect for the printed form. The books looked new. The jackets were clear of any stains. The pages were not creased. The only indication that these were used books was Zoe's name neatly printed on the first page and the message she left for the new owners. Some text was underlined and adorned with small hearts or sad faces. After going through half the books, Patricia gave up. She was disappointed, not sure what she was expecting to find. She placed the editions back in the trolley.

Patricia avoided calling Ken. She didn't know what to tell him, but she couldn't put it off any longer. She dialed their landline, hoping he'd be out, walking the dogs.

"Baldwin residence." He answered after three rings.

"Hi. Why aren't you walking Samson and Delilah?"

"Why would you call the house if you thought I was out. More importantly, why aren't you home yet?"

Patricia sighed, unsure how to answer.

"Pat, what's going on?"

"I don't know. I read the journals. I never knew she was so unhappy with her life. I simply assumed she was tired with all the traveling. The journals were full of anguish and bitterness. She agonized over a loss."

"You're not making any sense. What journals?"

"Zoe left three journals in the apartment, together with some books and her laptop. She mentioned a Mike and Oliver. I think one of them broke her heart."

"Your read her journals?"

"She discarded them."

"I doubt she thought they end up with you and that you would read them. Just come home."

"No, I have to talk to this Oliver and find out what happened."

"Pat, leave it alone. Don't go bothering this boy."

"But he'll know what happened."

"She's in Europe, like she said."

"We don't know that for sure. No, she's not Europe."

"Because of what you read?"

"Yes. Besides where is her furniture and clothes and …stuff? Why did she terminate her lease?"

"Pat…"

"I know this seems insane, but I'm sorry Ken, I can't come home until I know she's okay."

Patricia woke up early the next day. She went for a walk to clear her head and decided to go to Zoe's office and talk to her colleagues. She returned to the hotel, changed her cloths and called for a cab. She arrived at Freeport at ten thirty.

Fourteen months before, Zoe surprise her mother during the holiday season with news that she accepted a position as a project coordinator in New York for a regional Freight Forwarding company.

"But Zoe, you're a director at a global consultancy firm, isn't this a few steps down the corporate ladder?"

"I need a change. It's a really good company. It's a low stress environment and a low stress job."

"What about the money? It's definitely going to be much less than what you're currently making."

"The money's fine. Besides I don't need much."

"You'll be living in New York. I understand that the cost of living is quite expensive over there."

"I'll live on Long Island, not Manhattan."

"I just think it is such a waste, throwing away all those years with the firm."

The cab pulled up to a warehouse facility on Albany Avenue. A strong ocean scent overtook Patricia as she stepped out of the vehicle. The entrance to an office building was to the left of warehouse. Patricia walked up the pathway. She opened the door and stepped into a small vestibule. She tapped on the security glass of the second door and waited for the receptionist to buzzed her in.

"Hi, I'm Patricia Baldwin. I'd like to speak to someone from IT please."

"What is this in regards to?"

"My daughter Zoe Baldwin works here. If possible, I'd like to talk to her boss."

"How is Zoe? She was such a delightful young lady. She always stopped by my station to chat. We were all sad to see her go."

"Zoe's no longer with the company?"

"She resigned right before Christmas. Let me get Charles, he was Zoe's boss. Please have a seat."

Patricia sat in one of the available chairs. The receptionist whispered inaudibly into the handset for her telephone.

"He'll be right out." She told Patricia with a nervous smile.

A large man in his late forties, wearing khakis and a red polo shirt with the company's logo embroidered on the pocket, emerged a few minutes later. He greeted Patricia and escorted her to his office. They passed grey cubicles cordoned by pewter colored walls, a drop ceiling, and stained blue carpeting. There were no windows. Everyone was dressed in a similar fashion.

"Are you required to wear a uniform?" Patricia asked.

"Yes. Management believes it distills a sense of camaraderie and teamwork. There is no difference between white collars and blue collars. We all wear the same outfit because we're all on the same team." Charles beamed with pride as he delivered this speech.

Patricia had visited Zoe in Chicago at her old firm. Zoe had her own office, encased in glass paneling. Everyone dressed formally. Zoe had an affinity for dark suits. Observing the dull workstations, Patricia wondered why would Zoe accepted a job with this company.

"Ma'am, Angela tells me that you have some questions about Zoe."

"Yes. Why did she leave?"

"She said that she was going back to Chicago. She wanted to focus on her research work. I must say we were disappointed when she left. She was doing a wonderful job and worked very well with the rest of the team. Frankly, I was surprised when she accepted our offer. You know, with her qualifications and all."

"Could I talk to any of her colleagues?"

"I'm sorry ma'am, but may I ask why?"

"Zoe's missing. I was hoping to speak to her friends and figure out where she might be."

"I'm sorry to hear that. I don't know if Zoe made any friends. The only person I can think of is Melanie. She and Zoe shared a working space."

Melanie wasn't any help. She said that they didn't talk much. They occasionally discussed work or the weather. Other people gave different versions of Melanie's account. Zoe was quiet and discreet, but very competent and helpful. She kept to herself and always declined their invitation for a drink after work. Patricia lost hope after speaking to five employees. She thanked Charles and left. She called a cab and asked the driver to take her to the nearest Police station.

The Police told Patricia to wait a few weeks before filing a missing person report. If Zoe was in Europe, she should be back by then and get in touch with her mother. Patricia wasn't satisfied with this response and demanded that the on-duty sergeant post a notice with Zoe's description. She e-mailed him a picture of Zoe and left the station. She walked back to the hotel and called Ken.

"Something's wrong. I just know it. The police aren't going to do anything. I'm so frustrated. We must find her Ken. She's our daughter."

"Calm down Pat. I'm sure Zoe's fine. She's probably gotten a new job in the city and she's taken off to Europe to decompress before starting work. Come home."

"No. There was nothing about a new job in the journals. I am going to call Sylvia, maybe she knows what happened."

Zoe joined Wave Consultancy Services two years after moving to Chicago. Sylvia was a senior consultant on Zoe's team. They bonded over work and long weeks traveling to Phoenix, San Antonio, and Los Angeles. Zoe comforted Sylvia when she broke up with her boyfriend. She disapproved of her when they reconciled, and supported her when she finally terminated the relationship. Sylvia condoled Zoe when her grandmother died, and invited her to spend Christmas with her family the year Ken and Pat went on a cruise for the holidays. They became close friends. Zoe was Sylvia's Maid of Honor. She cried when Sylvia and her family moved to Washington. They stayed in touch. Zoe visited whenever she traveled to the East Coast.

"Hi Syl. This is Patricia Baldwin."

"Pat, it's been such a long time. How's Ken?"

"Good. Good. We're both good."

"How's Zoe? It's been almost a year since we last spoke."

"Oh? I was hoping you could tell me what was going with Zoe."

"What do you mean?"

They agreed to meet over the weekend.

Patricia boarded the 8:03 LIRR to Penn station Saturday morning. She took the N train from Herald square and exited at Prince Street. She was meeting Sylvia for breakfast. It was early morning but the Nolita area was bustling with young couples enjoying the exceptional sunny winter weather. Cafes were open for business. Most diners opted to occupy tables next to the window. Patricia peeked at them as she walked by. She foolishly searched for Zoe among the breakfast crowd. She hoped to see her dark chestnut curly hair. She examined the smiling faces for Zoe's dimpled chin and garnet brown eyes. But of course, Zoe wasn't there. She crossed Lafayette Street and walked to a deli on the corner. Patricia was early, she ordered herbal tea and waited for Sylvia to arrive.

They sat at a quiet table away from the counter. They ordered breakfast and talked until the food arrived. Patricia told Sylvia everything that occurred since receiving Jose's phone call six days before. She gave Sylvia an edited version of Zoe's journals.

"What do you think happened?" Asked Sylvia.

"I don't know. But, I'm sure she's not vacationing in Europe. I simply want to know that she's okay."

"Do you think she might've harmed herself?"

"I really don't know. My mind is saying that Zoe would never do anything like that. But I can't be sure, not after reading her journals. I was hoping you'd have some idea about what she was going through this past year."

"I don't know what to tell you Pat. Zoe and I didn't communicate that much. She stopped answering my calls. I offered to help her with the move and all, but she declined. I haven't seen her in over eighteen months."

"Who's Mike?"

"Mike was a mistake. I don't feel comfortable talking to you about this. If Zoe wanted you to know about him, she would have told you herself."

"Sylvia, you are a mother. You know how it feels to worry about your child. Please, I just want to find out where she is. Maybe this Mike guy might know what happened to her. They might be back together."

"I doubt that very much."

Sylvia reluctantly gave Patricia a detailed account of Mike and Zoe's relationship.

Zoe and Mike met at a conference in Dubai two years before. She was a keynote speaker on data trends in the retail industry. Mike approached her at the meet and greet following the discussion. He complimented her presentation. Zoe was passionate about her research. Her devotion was apparent when she talked about her work. Her voice pitched higher than normal, annotating and annunciating words. Her hands animated to further emphasis her rational. She drew in the audience and engaged them in the discussion whether an intimate group of five over dinner or a crowd of hundreds in an auditorium. Zoe inched further out of her reclusive shell when invited to deliver public speeches. She was most comfortable being isolated on a stage, the dark silhouette camouflaged the assembly. She was witty. She was knowledgeable. She was charming. She was herself. She tailored the context to fit the listeners. When lecturing university students, she used pop culture references. When presenting to clients, she cited journal studies and Gartner reports. Zoe was accustomed to people complimenting her performances and praising her confidence and mastery of the subject matter. She didn't like receiving public acclamation. It made her uncomfortable because she didn't know how to respond. Her natural reply to accolades was, "I'm simply doing my job." But people mistook this for arrogance. Over the years she perfected her social acknowledgement and learned to gracefully accept praise, then steer the conversation away from her and on to the topic at hand.

When Mike walked up to her that day at the conference, she was tired. She wished to retreat to her hotel room and rest. Zoe was jet lagged and craved sleep in the middle of the day. She developed a strong headache thirty minutes into her presentation. She smiled past the throbbing pain below her ponytail and skillfully maneuvered through the meet and greet. Mike approached her on the way to the elevator.

"Impressive presentation. How can you catalogue all of that information?" He asked.

"It's my job."

"I'm Mike by the way, Mike Toft from Kaufman Breigs." He extended his arm to shake hands.

"Zoe Baldwin. Nice to meet you."

"Maybe we could continue the discussion over dinner?"

The elevator arrived. Zoe held the door.

"I'm sorry, but I'm going to call it a day." She stepped into the elevator. Mike followed.

"I'm staying here as well. Maybe we can catch an early breakfast or a cup of coffee before the conference tomorrow. I'd really like to pick your brain on Big Data in Health Care." He gave her his business card. "I'm in room 2212."

Mike Toft worked out of Kaufman Breigs Boston office, a competing consultancy firm. He was six feet four inches tall, with wide broad shoulders. He had the body of a swimmer and a full head of perfectly coifed dark blonde hair. His green eyes were tightly tucked under his brow. He wore dark tailored suits with crisp white shirts and discrete colored ties. He was always clean shaven and well groomed. He was handsome and used his attractiveness to his advantage. He intimidated men with his height and intense glare. He seduced women with knowing smiles and attentive listening. The small curvature of his upper lip rendered his victims helpless to his gaze. Zoe and Mike knew of each other, although they had never met before. She was suspicious of his meeting request, yet agreed to an early breakfast. She suggested a meeting at 6 am. Zoe woke up at four to catchup on e-mails and hoped an early appointed would befuddle Mike and deter his defenses, enabling her to expose his true motives.

She arrived at the hotel's in-house restaurant at 5:56. Mike was already waiting for her. His face beamed with a broad smile as she entered. He stood up and greeted her with a firm hand shake. He towered over her. Waiters were setting up the breakfast buffet, nevertheless they accommodated Mike and Zoe.

"Thank you for meeting with me. I wasn't sure you'd come," he said.

"No problem. I must confess that I am intrigued," she replied.

He picked up a French press and poured her a cup and coffee. He topped it off with four ounces of nonfat milk. He knew Zoe's caffeine preference and breakfast regime. He had ordered warm cut steel oats with sliced bananas, honey, and cinnamon. He wanted to impress Zoe and she wanted to know why.

"Ms. Baldwin," he shook his head and smiled, "may I call you Zoe."

"Of course."

"Zoe, you know that Kaufman Breigs pioneered the use of Big Data for market analytics in consumer goods. We were able to standardize trend analysis across manufactures and retailers. Our portfolio of customers comprises of the biggest names from coast to coast. The partners at K&B are very impressed with your work in analytic algorithms. We'd like to extend your research to the Health Care industry."

He was attempting to recruit Zoe. She reclined in her chair and crossed her legs. She held the coffee cup to her lips and took short swift sips and silently ponder upon his words. Her face divulged nothing. She neither smiled nor frowned. She simply returned Mike's stare and considerately nodded on occasion. She remained silent, giving Mike the false sense that he had the upper hand in the conversation.

"We're aware that your forte in Big Data is a result of external studies. We're also aware that your current firm, WCS, doesn't take full advantage of your abilities. If I may say, you're being wasted in project management. We'd like to offer you a senior consultancy position with Kaufman Breigs. You'll have complete discretion in hiring your team. K&B's resources will be at your disposal. You'll have a choice to remain in Chicago or relocate to any of our offices nationwide. I'd personally prefer if you moved to Boston. I'd like for us to collaborate."

Zoe didn't respond. She put down the coffee cup and edged her seat closer to the table. She started to eat breakfast. Zoe deployed silence in negotiations to throw off her opponents. She'd observed them as their confidence rescinded. They'd fret about in their seats, tug at their facial hair or pull down their shirt cuffs. Zoe utilized these brief moments to process what has been said and plan her response. Uncomfortable with the silence, Mike reached across the table and touched her right hand.

"So Miss Baldwin, what do you think?"

Zoe had no desire to leave her firm. Although smaller than K&B, WCS's management allowed her enough flexibility to pursue her extra curricula activities in research and academic work. Had Zoe joined K&B, her life would have changed drastically. Short rapid business trips would have plagued her schedule. K&B required rigorous time keeping and billing records detailed in minutes. She would have to deal with the likes of Mike Toft on a daily basis. Zoe found Mike physically attractive. She admired his confidence. But she didn't trust him. Partner's at K&B were notorious for taking credit for others' work. Zoe would have to become as ruthless to survive and strive at K&B, to second guess everyone's motives, to shield her work and assume distrust in lieu of honesty. Zoe didn't enjoy working in such an environment. She finished her oatmeal and thanked Mike for his offer but graciously declined.

Three months after their encounter in Dubai, Mike left Zoe a voice mail. He was in Chicago and wanted to meet with her. She was surprised to hear from him. Never one to ruin a business relation, she returned his call.

"I haven't changed my mind about the job offer," she proclaimed over the phone.

"I'm not calling about that. I was thinking, maybe two friends could have dinner together. How about tomorrow, seven thirty at Basil and Tomato?"

Basil and Tomato was Zoe's favorite restaurant. It was within walking distance from her apartment. She frequently dined there. A husband and wife ran the cafe together. TJ was the chief and Maggie managed front of the house. Zoe enjoyed their gluten free pasta offering and fried calamari. They knew her by name and always had her order ready at precisely 5:25 pm. She picked it up on her way home. She agreed to meet him the next evening at six.

She arrived to find Mike waiting for her. He wore dark denim, a Burberry plaid shirt and brown suede jacket. He stood up to greet Zoe as she approached. He pulled out her chair.

"Are you always early for meetings?" Zoe asked.

"Only the one's that matter." He smiled.

"Mike, I feel bad about wasting your time, but I'm not interested in joining K&B."

"Fine, but would you be interested in leaving WCS?"

"I just said that I wasn't."

"No, you said you didn't want to work for K&B. I can understand that. K&B is a tough place. Not everyone is comfortable with that. But, this doesn't mean that you can't be convinced to leave WCS for something else." He sipped Pinot Noir and didn't alter his gaze away from Zoe.

"I am tough enough to handle K&B, it just doesn't factor in with my future plans."

"And WCS does?"

"Yes."

"As small as it is."

"Yes."

"Fair enough. So, what's good here?"

They ordered entrees and a main dish. They shared a bottle of wine and dessert. Mike explained that he temporarily relocated to Chicago to onboard a new client. He rented an apartment down the street from the restaurant. He didn't know anyone in Chicago and called her seeking company.

"You don't know anyone in Chicago, no one at all? That's somewhat hard to believe."

"Well, no one I'd like to dine with. They're mostly business acquaintances. I wanted a relaxing evening, to be with someone I'm comfortable around. You can understand that."

Zoe nodded as she drank coffee and signaled for the check.

"This one's on me. To welcome you to the neighborhood."

"You live around here?"

Zoe glanced at Mike through the narrow slits of her eyes, commanding him to cut the bullshit. He grinned smugly and apologized.

"Sorry, it's a habit. Researching my…um."

"Adversaries?"

He only smiled in response.

They exited Basil and Tomato together and walked along West Roslyn Place towards North Lakeview Avenue. Zoe pointed out various vendors in the area. She introduced Mike to the best dry cleaners. "They can get coffee stains out of anything," she proclaimed. She showed him where to buy fresh organic produce and the bars with the widest selection of beer on tap. She stopped in front of a ten-story bare brick building.

"This is me." She said, pointing to the structure. "Well, Mr. Toft, I had an enjoyable evening, surprisingly so." She reached out to shake his hand. He clasped her hand and leaned in. He kissed her good night on the cheek. A crimson tide flushed up Zoe's face. She was thankful for the dimly lit entrance. She rushed up the stairs to the lobby. She entered the building as Mike shouted, "Let's do this again, sometime soon." He left.

Zoe was attracted to Mike, but she pushed him out her mind. Yet, she couldn't escape him. Everyone at WCS was talking about Mike Toft moving to Chicago. He was being vetted to manage the entire east coast operations. He was in Chicago for eight months to rebuild their customer base. Younger female associates gossiped about his romantic conquests. He was cultivating a reputation of one-night stands.

"You have to stop stalking me like this." He teased her inline at Starbucks. He paid for her drink.

"Do you know Mike Toft?" Asked Molly.

"We met at a conference."

"Introduce me."

"Why?"

"Because he's hot."

"You do understand that I'm not his pimp."

She saw him around the neighborhood and at the deli during lunch time. They came across one another at competing proposals. One evening they exchanged text messages.

Free for dinner?

Yes.

B&T @ 6:00

Okay.

"Are you seeing anyone?" Zoe asked over vegetarian linguine.

"Why? Are you interested?"

"No. No. Someone at the office would like an introduction. Just thought I'd check first that you are available."

"Someone at the office?" He bemused.

*Smug son of a bitch.* Zoe thought. "Yes, Molly. She's the admin assistant at WCS. She was standing behind me at Starbucks. She's really nice and charming." She said. *This sounds moronic. How do people do this?* She wondered.

"Oh, her. How old is she, like twenty-two? Twenty-three?"

"Twenty-two. I think."

"So. that's what you think of me? That I only date twenty-two-year-olds."

"I'm not judging, just relaying a request. Don't shot the messenger."

"I'm very flattered but I'm interested in someone else at the moment."

"That was quick. Just a few weeks ago, you didn't have anyone to hang with in Chicago."

"Well. We knew each other before. We have been casually 'hanging out'. I think I'll ask her out on an official date."

"Good for you. I'm sure she's a lovely girl."

Mike paid for dinner and helped Zoe into her coat. He walked her to her building. He bent down to kiss her good night and whispered, "I'll pick you up Saturday at seven thirty."

Zoe was exuberant about her date with Mike. She incessantly had a sheepish smile plastered to her face, all week long. *Why are you so giddy?* She wondered. *Sure, Mike's handsome and charming, but he's also misogynistic and uses people for his own benefit. I can't believe that you're excited over a boy who likes you. It doesn't make sense, acting like teenagers. You should know better. You're delirious with lust. Do you want to sleep with him?* Zoe couldn't silence the dialogue in her head. She was apprehensive. She obsessed over her outfit. Trousers were too tight. Skirts were too short. Dresses made her look fat. Boots didn't compliment her calves. She finally opted for a solid black ensemble, her shield of armor. She selected fitted slacks, a dress shirt, and leather biker jacket. She wore red pumps and a patent red leather clutch. She bought red bordeaux lipstick for the occasion. She kept the rest of her makeup subdued. She mulled over her choice of perfume. Smiling slyly, she generously spritzed herself with fragrance. At precisely seven thirty, her phone buzzed with a text, I'm down stairs.

She let him wait for twenty minutes before emerging from the elevator. He was dressed in fitted jeans, accentuating his gluts, with a pale blue oxford shirt and navy cardigan with a shawl collar and wood buttons. His cologne filled the lobby. It overtook Zoe. A smile occupied his face.

"Interesting choice of color," he commented.

They walked two blocks to his apartment building. Zoe reluctantly entered as Mike held the door open.

"This seems highly inappropriate."

"I thought we'd be more relaxed in the privacy of my temporary home." he said.

"You've cooked dinner?" Zoe asked.

"Don't be ridiculous. I've had it delivered. It's warm and waiting."

After dinner Mike guided Zoe out to the terrace. His apartment was on the fifteen floor of a high-rise overlooking Lincoln Park.

"This view is amazing," she said.

"Finally, I've been trying to impress you ever since Dubai."

"Trust me, you don't need the view."

He grinned over the brim of his brandy tumbler. Zoe inhaled the fresh air. She closed her eyes and enjoyed the cool breeze of the bay against her face.

"May I ask you a question?" Mike asked.

"Of course."

He put down the glass and brushed is hand on his jeans. "Give me your hand."

Zoe skeptically unfolded her arm towards Mike. He ran his middle finger along the lines of her open palm and bent down. His nose grazed her wrist .

He looked up and asked, "What is that scent?"

"Would you believe me if I were to say it's my sweat."

"No."

"Mr. Toft, are you insinuating that my sweat stinks?"

"Do you ever just answer a question directly without smart comebacks."

Humbled with the confrontation, Zoe looked down at her feet. "Coco Mademoiselle. It's Coco Mademoiselle."

Mike bent down and took a final whiff. "It's quite enticing."

Zoe didn't leave Mike's apartment until the next morning. She woke up with a hickey above her left breast. It bothered her as she got dressed. She was uncomfortable while Mike skillfully bestowed it upon her. She was sore the next day, assumed from the lack of practice. She was a bit bruised from the passion. Their intercourse satisfied Zoe, for Mike was thoroughly competent. Yet, it was an exhibition of proficiency, void of intimacy. Mike was set on attaining the utmost sexual pleasure for himself and Zoe, in the most effective efficient manner. Emotions and sensuality were impediments. He brushed them aside as he executed his part with perfection. Zoe missed the intensity of desire.

Mike and Zoe's relationship progressed exponentially. They spent every night together. When either had to travel they stayed in touch over Skype. She was flatter that Mike wanted to be with her. Seducing and pleasing him made her feel feminine. Hearing his empty compliments made her feel beautiful. Their relationship developed in private. Zoe was hesitant to introduce Mike to her friends. She didn't mention him to her parents. She couldn't envision a future with Mike, not a future she desired. They didn't have much in common outside of work. The only topic to peak Mike's interest was Zoe's research. He'd ask her questions and urge her to leave WCS and focus on her studies. He only agreed to do activities he liked, sports events, sailing, and drinks at night clubs. Zoe enjoyed the evenings they stayed at home. She cooked dinner and they watched a movie. She missed her books. Yet, Mike kept her occupied. She didn't have enough time to read. They were driving to Buffalo one weekend. Zoe took advantage of the trip to read Mrs. Dalloway.

"Must you do that now?" asked Mike.

"We're just sitting in the car, doing nothing."

"What are reading anyway?" He looked over to the open page. "Really Zoe, you're reading the introduction." He reached for the book and tossed it on the back seat. "You have to listen to this new jazz band. I recorded them on my phone."

"I can read and listen simultaneously." Zoe was annoyed.

"That's disrespectful to the musicians."

Zoe spoke to Sylvia about her doubts regarding Mike.

"No woman in her right mind would let Mike Toft go. Are you insane? You're just picking at nothing. If he makes managing partner at K&B, his income is going to be seven figures. Need I say the word? He's a catch." Sylvia said.

"I know all of that."

"So what's the problem exactly?"

"I can't picture myself with him. He's indifferent and blasé. He lacks empathy and goodwill."

"What do you mean?"

"He exploits weaknesses in others, including me. I can't be vulnerable around him."

"Zoe, no man is going to be perfect or exactly as you imagine him in your head. Relationships are about making compromises. Every human being is a combination of good and bad. You have to accept them for what they are, work with the bad to savor the good."

"What's so good about Mike?"

"He's there. He's sticking around, and he loves you."

"He never said that."

"He doesn't have to say the words 'I love you' to express his feelings. He is faithful, he supports your research. He wants you to live together. He loves you."

"I want to move in with him. It's not the same things as living together."

"Zoe, I'm sure there are things about you that bother him."

"Yes, there are and he's been very vocal about them. He thinks I should dress more femininely and wear more skirts. He wants me to grow out my hair and loose at least fifteen pounds. He wants five children Sylvia, five."

"You've always wanted a family."

"Not five kids."

"The good with the bad Zoe. That's all we can do."

"So, basically Mike's the best I can do?"

"Trust me, you can do much worse than Mike Toft. Zoe, you've been lonely for a long time. Mike is offering you something you want, companionship. Every relationship comes at a price. You have to decide if being with Mike is worth it or not."

Zoe wondered if she was depriving herself the joy of a relationship because she was holding out for something impossible. She focused on Mike's flaws and neglected to see him as a man, as a life partner. People often commented on her lack of love life. Her parents, friends, and distant relatives imparted unwarranted romance wisdom. She was too career focused. She wasn't attractive enough. She intimidated men. She read too much. Zoe wondered if there was any truth to these arbitrary intrusive analysis. Maybe Zoe had unrealistic expectations. If everyone believed that Mike Toft was the perfect man, there must be some legitimacy to this claim. Zoe deliberated and contemplated her alternatives. She decided to bury her doubts about Mike's lapse of character deep in her consciousness and to concede to his wishes to change her appearance. She was thirty-six and never had a serious relationship. She must have been doing something wrong, it's only rational. She was no less of a woman for submitting to her man's desires. She reduced her office hours at WCS and shifted her attention to research work. She accepted Mike's offering of two dresser drawers and shared closet space. She moved in with him, but kept her condo. They officially became a couple. She introduced him to her friends and colleagues as her boyfriend.

Zoe conducted the majority of her research from Mike's den. He surprised Zoe with an unexpected gift. He presented her with a sleek glass and steel desk for a working space. Her research associates often dropped by with documents and papers. Mike insisted they stay for dinner. He was a considerate and entertaining host. He remembered their names and favorite drinks. Gabriella, a post graduate associate working on her masters, lingered at the apartment more than necessary. She assisted Zoe on devising an algorithm to extrapolate behavioral patterns. Gaby's Latin heritage endowed her with a dark smooth complexion. She was five feet nine inches tall, with long limbs and an elongated body. Her immaculate muscle definition was due to a disciplined yoga and Pilates routine. Gaby kept her straight blond hair in a loose French braid, highlighting her heavily lashed olive eyes and symmetric face.

Mike and Gaby engaged in lively discussions about Jazz and NCAA Football. Gaby supported UCB's Colorado Buffaloes, Mike's alma mater. In pseudo-hushed tones Gaby confessed to knowing very little about sailing, as Mike explained the difference between sailing the Great Lakes and Cape Code. Gaby was attracted to Mike. Most women fell victim to his charms. However, Mike was more than charming, he was flirtation and lavished women with flattery.

Zoe's insecurities delivered boisterous warning signals. She confronted Mike.

"I was just being nice to her because you guys work together. Sorry. It won't happen again."

Zoe was enraged when she discovered Mike had invited Gaby to go sailing with his friends. She asked him to cease all contact. Their tumultuous cohabitation lasted from February through July. For one hundred and eighty-six days, Zoe denied her doubts and quieted her fears. Most women faced the plight of taming men. She too was obligated to endure the same. Relationships are complicated with the gravity of integrating two lives and two personalities. The harder it is to develop and sustain a relationship, the stronger the bond.

\*\*\*

Zoe returned to the apartment one afternoon in August. She walked in the living room and found Sara, Mike's personal assistant, waiting for her. She was sitting at the breakfast bar next to Zoe's two suitcases. She was on the phone. She looked up as Zoe approached. Her crimson lips curved upwards in a fictitious smile. Her red lacquered finger tips held a letter from Mike.

*Babe,*

*Sorry to do this, like this, but I have to vacate the place by the end of the week. Sara will take care of everything.*

*Luv,*
*Mike*

"What does this mean?" Zoe asked Sara.

"Mr. Toft is moving back to Boston. He's been appointed as Regional Managing Director. His replacement is arriving Monday. We have to get the place ready. I packed your things. A car is waiting for you down stairs." She arched her eyebrows to inquire if Zoe had any further questions.

"Right. Thank you."

"I'll give you a moment."

Sara waited on the balcony, occupied with her phone. Zoe called Mike. He didn't answer. She left him a voice message, "What the fuck? Call me."

Zoe returned to her condo. The air was stale. She turned on all the lamps and opened all the windows, hoping the light would help her comprehend what had happened. Mike didn't mention Boston or the promotion to her. She was confused. *Did Mike expect me to move to Boston? What about my job and research? Will I end up a housewife, like Sylvia?* She wondered. Mike called her that evening.

"Hi babe. What's up?" He asked.

"What's up? Where are you?"

"I'm at Logan International."

"You're in Boston?"

"Yes."

"Mike, what's going on?"

"They offered me the job and I accepted?"

"When did this happen?"

"Last week."

"Why didn't you tell?"

"Because it was confidential and you work for a competitor, a small firm, but a competitor nonetheless."

"When do you start?"

"I'm on my way to meet a new client."

"So you've already started."

"Yes."

"What about us?"

"Babe it was fun, but now it is over."

"Over?"

"Zoe, don't be like this. What we had was symbiotic. You were lonely and I was alone. We kept each other company. Besides, you always knew that Chicago was a temporary situation for me."

"And I was a part of that situation."

"I never said anything to the contrary."

"I thought you cared, that you wanted to be with me." Zoe audibly cried. Sobs escaped as she hiccupped between breaths.

"Zoe, please don't cry. Of course I care about you. I was with you because I wanted to."

"But not anymore? I can move to Boston. I can take that job with Kaufman Breigs. I can shift my research to UMASS."

Mike sighed.

"Say something," Zoe told him.

"We'd love to have you at Kaufman Breigs, but don't do this for me. It'll still be over, even if you move to Boston."

"Why?"

"I don't want to do this in the airport."

"Then you should have talked to me before leaving. I deserve an explanation."

"Look, we had a good time together and now it's over. What else is there to explain?"

"I thought you loved me."

"I never said that."

"Why?"

"Why what?"

"Why can't you love me?"

"Zoe, you're better than this."

"Just tell me why. What is so unlovable about me?"

"Goodbye Zoe."

"So, you see Patricia, Zoe would never return to Mike." Explained Sylvia.

"She never mentioned any of this."

"She was ashamed. She couldn't face you with such a failure hanging over her."

"I'm her mother."

"But you expected so much of her. She didn't want to disappoint you."

"I thought I was being supportive of her choices, of her career. Is this why she left Chicago?"

"Being with Mike gave her a new perspective on belonging. She couldn't go back to her old life. She wanted something different, but she didn't know what. She hoped to find it in New York."

"But that job was beneath her. She could have done better."

"She was tired, both physically and emotionally. She lost motivation. The new job was easy. It didn't require much mental effort from her. The few times we communicated while she was in New York, she seemed happy. Pat, I sincerely believe that Zoe has gone off somewhere to clear her mind. I'm certain she's fine and will contact you soon."

"Thank you Sylvia. But I'm not going to wait to find out. I have to know for sure."

"What are you going to do?"

"I'm going to speak to this Oliver Scott. Maybe he knows what happened."

Patricia came across Oliver's business card while going through Zoe's belongs. She called him. A dial tone gave away to voice mail. Patricia left a message explaining who she was and asking Mr. Scott to call her back. She left her cell number. Oliver failed to comply. After two uneventful attempts to contact him, Patricia was able to reach Oliver. He agreed to meet her the next day.

Patricia woke up early to prepare for their meeting. Oliver didn't seem to know who she was. He was formal and polite, referring to her as Mrs. Baldwin. They were meeting at his office in Columbia. Patricia packed Zoe's journals in her pocket book. Following Zoe's instructions, Patricia boarded the LIRR to Penn station then switched to the One train. She exited at A Hundred and Sixteenth Street. Patricia heard Zoe's voice describing the landscape she frequented during the previous summer months. She retraced Zoe's footsteps. She got coffee from the Starbucks on Broadway. She walked the familiar paths of Morningside campus. She climbed the stairs of Philosophy Hall and walked to Oliver's office. He was waiting for her. He stood up and stepped out from behind the desk to greet her at the door and offered her a seat. Unbeknownst to Patricia, she selected the same seat Zoe did last June. Oliver closed the door, warranting them privacy. He walked the five paces to his desk and sat down. The strong scent of cigarettes, breath mints and vanilla air fresher overwhelmed Patricia. She suspected that Oliver smoked inside the office. The window to Patricia's right was left ajar, despite the fridge weather of February.

"Well, Mrs. Baldwin, what brings you to New York?" He asked.

"Please, call me Patricia."

"Patricia. How is Zoe?"

"I was hoping you could tell me."

"I beg your pardon."

"Zoe is missing. I was hoping you might know where she is, given the nature of your relationship."

"I haven't seen Zoe in over five months. I have no idea where she could possibly be."

There were no traces of concern in his demeanor. *How cruel*, Patricia thought. *Has he moved on already? Did he break Zoe's heart?* Patricia silently observed Oliver.

"Is there anything else I can do for you, Patricia?" Oliver asked.

He got up indicating the end of the meeting. She ignored his maneuver. She was dissatisfied with this answer.

"What went wrong? Why did you and Zoe stop seeing each other? Her journals end so abruptly. They offer no explanations."

"It was a limited research engagement. We initially agreed to three months, but it lagged a bit longer. Zoe didn't object to the extension. The work was done and Zoe was compensated for her efforts."

"What? I don't understand."

"My book. Once it was completed, I no longer needed her services. She agreed to these terms."

"Yes, but why did you break up?"

"Mrs. Baldwin, Zoe and I were never involved romantically. We had a professional relationship. We chatted and dined together a couple of times, within the course of our work. But that was the extent of our interactions. I am fond of Zoe. She is intelligent and obviously very competent in her line of work. I considered her a friend, but never a lover. Never."

"Why are you denying your relationship with her?"

"There's nothing to deny."

"That's not what she wrote in her journals."

"Mrs. Baldwin, I'm not sure what your motives are. I assure you, Zoe and I were strictly colleagues. I must ask you to leave. I only have a few minutes to prepare for my next lecture."

With these words Oliver extended his arm to shake Patricia's hand and prompt her to leave. She reached in her purse and retrieved the colorfully bounded journals, encased filaments of Zoe's consciousness.

"I have been puzzling over the reason why Zoe left these behind. Whether the events described on these pages are true or fantasy, I think you should have them."

She placed the books on Oliver's desk and left.

Ken called Patricia to let her know that he was at JFK airport and he'd be at the hotel in thirty minutes. His voice solaced Patricia. She waited in the lobby. The ten days she spent in New York reading the journals, tracing Zoe's movements, and meeting Charles, Sylvia, and Oliver drained her emotionally and physically. She cried with relief upon seeing Ken walk into the hotel, pulling his carryon behind him. He sheltered his wife's tears in an embrace. He let her weep in peace.

"I'm happy you came," she said as they held hands.

Patricia and Ken had dinner at a local pizzeria. After the waiter seated them and took their order, Ken confessed that he, too, was concerned about Zoe. He hired a private detective who ran Zoe's passport number. She hadn't gone through border control for the past year.

"She hasn't left the country. She's definitely not in Europe, that's for sure. There hasn't been any movement on her credit cards for the last five weeks. The detective thinks she using cash, but she can't book flights or hotel rooms without a credit card. There are no pending transactions on her cards," Ken said.

"What does this mean?" Patricia asked.

"He thinks she's still in the country, hiding somewhere. Do you have her laptop?"

"Yes. Why?"

"He wants to check her internet search history. He might be able to pick-up some clues from websites she visited. He's in New York, out in Queens, working on another case. He'll meet us tomorrow in the hotel."

"Why didn't you tell me about the detective?"

"I begged you to come home."

"That doesn't answer my question."

"I was waiting to have something worth telling, but nothing definite has surfaced."

Distraught with her own concern for Zoe, Patricia neglected to notice Ken's weary and tired appearance. She didn't acknowledge his pain. His face sunk with the burden of not knowing where Zoe was. He's shoulder slanted with the possibility that she was harmed. He smiled at his wife to maintain his strong disposition. He smiled to conceal his inability to rescue his little girl. The recollection of Zoe lacerated his heart, but he couldn't cry for his daughter. What good would tears do. Ken resorted to pragmatic actions. Yet, he toiled over Zoe's fate. Patricia selfishly remained in New York isolating them both from one another, when they need each other the most. She held Ken's hand firmly in her palms.

"The detective thinks Zoe's mixed up with drugs or alcohol. He says she'll resurface in a few weeks."

"What?" Patricia protested to the thought of her daughter as an addict.

"I know it's insane. He's checking Zoe's bank accounts for suspicious withdrawals."

"I suppose it won't do any harm to check."

Zoe formatted her laptop and installed a fresh copy of the operating system. The device was operational, but it didn't contain any data. The detective retrieved the security footage from the apartment building on South Park. The camera in the lobby showed Zoe walking out at 5:20 am on Tuesday, 28th January. It was the last footage of her. It was in black and white. The detective couldn't discern her outfit.

"She was dressed in dark pants, possibly jeans, and a dark grey jacket. It could be any color from brown to olive. She had on a grey color scarf and cap. She wasn't carrying a purse or bag."

He showed Pat and Ken the footage. They looked at the image of Zoe pausing before the large glass panels to pull on her mittens before stepping out.

"Is this all you could find?" Asked Ken.

"I checked the footage from the camera on the third floor, right outside her door. There was nothing unusual in the week leading up to the twenty eighth. There's footage of Zoe taking out large garbage bags. She took them down to the basement. But that's normal, if she was moving out of the place. However, I saw no furniture or luggage being removed from the premises. I have no idea how she got them out of the apartment."

"Can we check with the garbage collectors or landfills to find out what was in those bags?" Patricia asked.

"Ma'am, it's been almost a month, I'm sure the bags have been disposed of by now."

"What else can we do?"

"Well, I've checked her phone records. There wasn't a lot of activity on the line, mostly data consumption, but nothing major. She made a couple of calls to a Sylvia Channing, a 202 number."

"She's Zoe's friend."

"The other calls were made to your landline and then a bunch of text messages to an Oliver Scott."

"Zoe worked with him."

"At Columbia University?"

"Yes, she was doing some research work."

"In English literature?"

"Yes."

The detective raised his eyebrows and replied, "Well, that's it. I couldn't retrieve the content of these messages, but I can have a talk with Mr. Scott."

"That won't be necessary. I have already spoken to him. He doesn't know where Zoe is. What do we do next?"

"Mrs. Baldwin, your daughter went through extreme lengths to disappear and not be found. That's something you need to realize and just."

"What? Give up."

"No, give in. Give in to Zoe's wishes to be left alone."

"I'm sorry but I can't do that."

"I'm afraid there's nothing else we can do at this point. I understand that you have posted a missing person's report with the police."

"Yes." Ken answered.

"All you can do is wait." The detective replied.

No words condoled Patricia. She had let Zoe down. She hoped her daughter had retreated to happiness, seeking a new beginning, away from all the Mikes and Olivers. Patricia closed her eyes and conjured up an image of her daughter's smiling face. She saw a six-year-old Zoe on the swing set in their backyard. Her brown curly pigtails flapped in the air as she swung high. She giggled with each leg stroke. She was fearless. She tethered to the rubber seat and laid back, almost completely flat, and pushed the swing down. Patricia searched for an adult Zoe in her memories. She only saw a hallow image in a business suit, wearing a formal smile. *Where did the happy little girl go? When did I fail Zoe?* Patricia wondered, but she couldn't find any comfort. She knew that she'll never see Zoe again.

Patricia wanted to do one last thing before leaving for Charlotte. She packed Zoe's books into the shopping trolley and took them into Manhattan. Patricia and Ken visited all the locations that Zoe wrote about in her journal. They left behind a trail of stories. Zoe found solace and solitude in her books. She also found sanctum in Bryant Park, the High Line, Lincoln Centre, Morningside Park, and Washington Square. Patricia left a book on every bench and table, hoping someone else will find comfort in them, secretly wishing her daughter would visit these places and find her books. They'd guide Zoe to a place of safety and sanity. With the thud of each book placed throughout the city, Patricia said a silent prayer for Zoe with her tears and a farewell with her heart.